EVALUATION ESSENTIALS

EVALUATION ESSENTIALS

Methods for Conducting Sound Research

BETH OSBORNE DAPONTE, Ph.D.

JOSSEY-BASS
A Wiley Imprint
www.josseybass.com

Published by Jossey-Bass
A Wiley Imprint
989 Market Street, San Francisco, CA 94103—www.josseybass.com

Readers should be aware that Internet Web sites offered as citations or sources for further information may have changed or disappeared since time this was written.

Limit of Liability/Disclaimer of Warranty: While the publisher and author have used their best efforts in preparing this book, they make no representations or warranties with respect to the accuracy or completeness of the contents of this book and specifically disclaim any implied warranties of merchantability or fitness for a particular purpose. No warranty may be created or extended by sales representatives or written sales materials. The advice and strategies contained herein may not be suitable for your situation. You should consult with a professional where appropriate. Neither the publisher nor author shall be liable for any loss of profit or any other commercial damages, including but not limited to special, incidental, consequential, or other damages.

Jossey-Bass books and products are available through most bookstores. To contact Jossey-Bass directly call our Customer Care Department within the United States at (800) 956-7739, outside the United States at (317) 572-3986, or via fax at (317) 572-4002.

Jossey-Bass also publishes its books in a variety of electronic formats. Some content that appears in print may not be available in electronic books.

Library of Congress Cataloging-in-Publication Data

Daponte, Beth Osborne, 1962–
    Evaluation essentials : methods for conducting sound research / Beth Osborne Daponte. — 1st ed.
      p. cm.
    Includes bibliographical references and index.
    ISBN 978-0-7879-8439-7 (pbk.)
      1. Evaluation research (Social action programs)   2. Social sciences—Methodology.
   I. Title.
   H62.D236   2008
   001.4—dc22

                                           2008007629

Printed in the United States of America
FIRST EDITION

PB Printing   10 9 8 7 6 5 4 3 2 1

CONTENTS

FIGURES AND TABLES

FIGURES

TABLES

PREFACE

This book was motivated by my frustration that there did not seem to be a text already on the market that delves into *all* of the issues that evaluators today confront. When teaching program evaluation, I would have my students purchase two to four books (one on evaluation processes, one on quasi-experimental design, one introducing survey design, and another on literature reviews!) and obtain countless articles to use as resources for the class. Lectures and working with clients would tie the material together.

In this book, all of the evaluation issues that an evaluator must think through are covered. The book instructs how to rigorously describe programs and provides examples of program descriptions. It discusses what it means to say that a program "causes" change to occur. It provides a rigorous introduction to quasi-experimental design, allowing the reader to determine which designs are suitable for a given situation and understand the trade-offs between designs. The book provides an introduction to data collection, sketching out the pros and cons of various approaches. Further, the text discusses how to conduct effective literature reviews and the relationship between evaluation and proposal writing.

I have two hopes for the text. First, that it be used as a springboard for instructors to provide a rigorous course in evaluation. By relying on the text, students will be assured that their program evaluation course covers all of the basics. Instructors interested in delving into any area in more detail or in topical areas should supplement the text with journal articles or timely studies.

Second, many working in the nonprofit arena today did not have the opportunity to take a rigorous course in evaluation during their training. In addition, more senior people in the nonprofit arena have seen an emphasis shift toward evaluation. I hope that this book provides them with a valuable resource and gets them up to speed on the evaluation arena.

ACKNOWLEDGMENTS

Many people helped in the creation of this book. My students have always inspired me. It is through working with them over the years that I have resolved how to best approach and teach program evaluation. Former students Greg Lagana, Rick Cain, Shannan Bade, Gary Margolis, and Nitin Madhav were exceptionally inspirational.

However, had it not been for the faculty of the H. John Heinz School of Public Policy and Management at Carnegie Mellon University, I may not have felt confident enough to branch out into the field of evaluation. Many years ago, Al Blumstein, while dean, convinced me that my demographic skills and the rigor of the graduate training I received at the University of Chicago would make me a good teacher of program evaluation. It was there that I first taught program evaluation. Colleagues at the University of Pittsburgh, namely Ann Farber and Deborah Stark, showed me the importance of the non-quantitative aspects of evaluation and developing skills to work with community-based organizations. Conversations with them were invaluable in my growth in this field. They proved to me the importance of truly getting to know a program before one can determine how to evaluate it. Over the years, I have refined the course. Now, I think that it carefully balances all of the skills that a student of evaluation should possess. In the course, I match small groups of students with local organizations and businesses and have the students design a very detailed evaluation plan for their "clients." I have learned a tremendous amount working with my students and these organizations.

I am indebted to the numerous nonprofits that have opened their souls up to me and my students. Joyce Rothermel, executive director of the Greater Pittsburgh Community Food Bank, and Ken Regal, co-director of Just Harvest, have shown me how effective nonprofits can be. They are truly exceptional leaders for their respective organizations and are perfect examples of "inputs that cannot be replicated but must be listed" in program logic models.

I am grateful for having had the pleasure of working with two courageous leaders who, in very different ways, pushed their respective organizations to use meaningful data and an evaluatory approach. Doug O'Brien, who recently transitioned from America's Second Harvest to lead the Vermont Food Bank, showed me how research and data can keep issues alive. Lillian Cruz of The Community Foundation for Greater New Haven has pushed her organization to use an evaluation approach in its quest to continuously improve.

I am especially grateful to Jay Kadane, emeritus of Carnegie Mellon University for encouraging me to write this book. Colleagues at the Institution for Social and Policy Studies gave me the space and time to write. I am indebted to Don Green and Pam Greene for their support. Further, Geri Spadacenta, as always, provided exceptional administrative support.

My children are just beginning to understand what life is like without their mother writing a book, and I am grateful to them for their support. My husband, Tony Smith Jr., always supports what I do and this endeavor was no exception.

Finally, had it not been for the dual encouragement and vast amounts of patience from Andy Pasternak at Jossey-Bass, this book certainly would not have come to fruition. I am especially grateful to him for his role in making this book a reality.

THE AUTHOR

Beth Osborne Daponte, Ph.D., is a senior research scholar at the Institution for Social and Policy Studies and lecturer in the School of Management at Yale University. She has taught program evaluation for fifteen years. She started her career in evaluation at Carnegie Mellon University and at the University Center for Social and Urban Research at the University of Pittsburgh. She received her Ph.D. from the Social Sciences Division of the University of Chicago, Department of Sociology, specializing in demography.

Dr. Daponte has worked with a wide variety of nonprofit, governmental, and for-profit organizations, helping them to overcome their evaluation challenges. Currently, she is working with a large community foundation, helping to address its evaluation challenges at both the organizational and programmatic levels. Beyond evaluation, Dr. Daponte has conducted research in the fields of population estimation and food assistance, and worked as a policy coordinator for Ned Lamont for Senate. Her recent publications focus on food assistance to the poor. She has published in journals including the *Nonprofit and Voluntary Sector Quarterly,* the *Journal of the American Statistical Association,* the *American Journal of Public Health,* and the *Journal of Human Resources.* She resides in Stratford, Connecticut with her husband and three children.

EVALUATION ESSENTIALS

CHAPTER

INTRODUCTION

*The role of the program director is to believe,
the role of the evaluator is to doubt.*

—Carole Weiss

LEARNING OBJECTIVES

After reading this chapter, you should be able to

- Explain the primary and secondary goals of evaluation
- Describe the steps of the evaluation framework

An executive director of a medium-sized, nonprofit social service agency once told me, "I know we're doing good—I can see it in our clients' eyes." I wish that this was a unique encounter, but I have repeatedly had people responsible for running programs and delivering services to clients tell me some version of the above statement. Sometimes there is a variation on the statement—"Funders wouldn't fund us if we weren't doing good," or from the funders' perspective, "They must have done something good since they spent all of the money in the way that they said they were going to." Sometimes, administrators view increases in program enrollment as evidence of program success.

Unfortunately, none of these statements tells us what would have occurred to clients if the program hadn't been in existence. Clients may have been just as successful, or even more successful, if left to their own devices.

In all fairness, if those who deliver services didn't believe that they were effectively improving people's lives, they might have trouble delivering the services. It is difficult to devote oneself to a job if one doesn't believe that one's efforts have a positive effect.

The primary job of the evaluator is to examine rigorously the impact of interventions. However, a secondary job is to persuade those who believe that they can determine their effectiveness by looking into their clients' eyes to be more critical of the role that their services play in their clients' lives. Although clients' eyes may reflect gratitude, they cannot reveal whether a program reaches its intended **target population,** or whether clients would have been just as well off without the program. A critical perspective is needed if the efforts are to continually improve over time.

We are at a cusp of change in the way that programs are funded and delivered. Governmental funding, even for the most basic needs such as housing and food, is drying up, and more reliance is being placed on the nonprofit sector. Increasingly, government is relying on the nonprofit sector, with its army of volunteers and relatively low-paid staff, to compensate for gaps in governmental programs. This became painfully evident during the aftermath of Hurricane Katrina, when short-term federal assistance seemed ineffective, and government officials asked Americans to donate to a host of nonprofit organizations for hurricane aftermath relief initiatives because the federal government did not provide enough support to meet the tremendous need that developed.

However, with more reliance placed on the nonprofit sector comes the demand for all nonprofit organizations (also known in the international context as nongovernmental organizations or NGOs), and especially those that compete with other nonprofits for "market share," to demonstrate their effectiveness. This demand derives from many sources. First, government and consumers would like to know which nonprofits are most effective at providing comparable services. In this respect, evaluation is viewed as essentially a means of providing information to rank programs and organizations. Second, there exists curiosity about the ultimate effectiveness of services and programs; in this regard, evaluation is used to determine which approaches are the most appropriate for remedying a problem or for bringing about change.

Although well trained in service delivery, many in the nonprofit world lack training in the nuances of evaluation research. Likewise, many in the funding world who have "caught the evaluation bug" lack the background to determine how to form fair criteria by which to judge and reward effective nonprofit organizations and programs.

Working in the background behind service deliverers and funders are people who call themselves evaluators. Many evaluators are primarily trained in a field other than evaluation, such as public health, sociology, economics, statistics, or public policy. They may have had some formal training in evaluation, but they often have moved into evaluation over time (sometimes because of job and market demands) and many have acquired mostly on-the-job training. For this reason, although the majority of evaluators have in common a desire to learn the "truth" about interventions, they bring to the table a divergent set of skills and may place varying emphases on different aspects of programs, policies, and evaluatory practices.

My perspective is aligned with that of Michael Quinn Patton (1996)—the goal of evaluation is to assist with continuous programmatic improvement and introspection. I readily acknowledge that how to achieve this goal is more of an art than a science. However, there is a rigor to the art and there exist tools that the artist needs to have in order to create the most appropriate evaluatory approach for the intervention at hand. Like a painter, the evaluation artist needs to understand the context and size of the canvas. Then, the artist needs to apply colors to the canvas that will result in a pleasing picture.

THE EVALUATION FRAMEWORK

The box below displays (in a very condensed form) the broad steps one must go through to successfully develop an evaluation of a program. All of these issues are discussed throughout the remainder of this book.

THE EVALUATION FRAMEWORK

1. Are the evaluation activities formative or summative?
2. What questions are in the universe of possible evaluation questions?
3. Rigorously describe the program by developing the program theory and using a program logic model.
4. Revisit and narrow the universe of evaluation questions.
5. Develop the evaluation plan.
6. Develop a data collection and data analysis plan.
7. Analyze the data.
8. Write evaluation report.

1. Are the evaluation activities formative or summative? Summative evaluations answer the question "What was the impact of what was done?" whereas formative evaluation addresses the question "How can the program improve what it does?"

2. Determine the possible universe of evaluation questions. Before engaging in any evaluation activities, you should determine the universe of possible evaluation questions, based on informal interviews conducted with program stakeholders.

3. Rigorously describe the program. Next, you must describe the program by diagramming its *program theory* (also known as the *theory of change*) and charting out its *program logic model*. These two tools force evaluators to become acquainted with the program, both theoretically and operationally. Many evaluators skimp on learning what the program is all about. I contend that any evaluation that is done without a thorough understanding of the program can be of no constructive use. For this reason, I devote a considerable portion of this book to getting to know the program.

With respect to the program theory, helping program personnel to articulate how they expect change to occur as a result of their program's activities can be quite revealing. Often, personnel have differing views on how and to what extent these changes will occur. Getting everybody on the same page can be a very time-consuming endeavor, and it can take a considerable amount of time for consensus to be reached, but the explication of the program theory ultimately allows the program to operate in a more focused way.

Diagramming the causal chain of the program theory helps you to consider whether, theoretically, the program can have an impact. The program theory also encourages better understanding of which parts of the chain are unknown and thus ripe for research, and which parts of the chain are so based in fact or on proven relationships that it is not necessary to examine or prove that particular link. For example, even though the goal of a program that distributes prescription drugs to low-income people might be improved health, the program does not need to show that taking the drugs under a prescribed protocol improves health—that relationship is known and proven. Instead, the evaluation of the program might focus on the processes utilized to increase drug access to the low-income population.

A well-constructed program logic model reveals strengths and potential weaknesses within the program. Although some program administrators are reluctant to streamline or focus a program, there is value in tightening up a program based on the program logic model. By tightening up a program, I mean slashing anything extraneous from the program logic model. All goals should have activities tied to them; all assumptions should reflect reality; the target population should be described as narrowly as possible; appropriate activities should be in place so that goals are achievable; and the program should have access to enough resources in order to function.

Sometimes, program directors roll up their sleeves and approach an evaluation intending to conduct a full-blown outcome-based quasi-experimental evaluation. However, once the program logic model and program theory are displayed, administrators may want to and sometimes should be encouraged to tweak or revamp the program if they see room for improvement. Rethinking the program should not be perceived negatively.

Seen under the harsh lights of a program logic model, a program may need to be reworked in order to be effective and the outcome-based evaluation may be put off until the program is stable.

4. Revisit and narrow the evaluation questions. After rigorously describing the program, evaluators should revisit the universe of evaluation questions and narrow them accordingly. Program administrators and funders should be open to the idea that outcome-based evaluation is not the only type of evaluation that could bring about program improvements. Process-oriented evaluation can also be fruitful. In fact, for unstable programs, process-based rather than outcome-based evaluation will be appropriate.

5. Develop an evaluation plan. It is not until the program is rigorously described that one can plan an appropriate evaluation. Certainly, the appropriate evaluation framework cannot be determined from the program title alone. I once became familiar with a program known as the "Class-Size Reduction Program." From the title, one might have expected the number of children in the classroom at any given time to have been reduced by the program. However, this interpretation of the program's activities would have been incorrect. Instead of reducing class size, the program provided a participating classroom with a teacher's aide for about four hours per week. At no point was the number of students in the classroom reduced. In fact, the program increased the number of people in the classroom. After seeing a program rigorously described using a program logic model and program theory, the appropriate evaluation questions and approaches become readily apparent.

Before deciding on an outcome-based evaluation, you should ask the following questions:

- Is the program stable?

- Are the services delivered as intended?

If the answer to either of these questions is "no," then you would certainly examine the processes of the program and put an outcome-based evaluation on hold, at least for now. There would be no point in examining outcomes other than, perhaps, collecting baseline data on the population served.

If you choose to examine *processes* (which would be the case in the event that the program is not stable), then you need to develop a feedback system that would determine not only the extent to which the program is being implemented appropriately and as intended, but also how to use the information on program processes.

If using an outcome-based evaluation approach, you must then decide which outcome measures are most appropriate. After consensus is reached on the relevant measures, the next consideration is which *quasi-experimental design* would best demonstrate that the program actually *causes* changes to occur. The question of what would have occurred to participants if the program did not exist is paramount in this decision; evaluators must be thinking of a "but for" statement—"but for this program, how participants would have fared." The quasi-experimental stage considers relevant "control groups" and the ethics of collecting information from those who are not receiving the benefits of a program.

6. Develop a data collection plan. This part of the evaluation plan describes how data will be collected, whether by using primary data collection techniques such as focus groups, interviews, or surveys, or by relying on secondary or pre-existing sources, such as census or archival program data.

If a survey is chosen to collect data, then you need to design and pre-test the survey, come up with a sampling schema, and then implement the survey. If other data collection approaches are used, then you need to consider a data collection protocol so only relevant data are extracted. For example, if client records are available but only a few outcome measures will be used, then the evaluation needs to develop a protocol so that only the relevant information is extracted from the records.

7. Decide how data will be analyzed. You also should consider which types of statistical techniques are most appropriate. There are countless decisions to be made when collecting and analyzing data. Sometimes, findings that result from an evaluation are not robust to the analysis approach and methods used. That is, if a different statistical approach was used, the results could change.

This overall decision model must be followed in order to determine the appropriate approach and criteria for evaluation, and I contend that it is impossible to determine these ahead of time. For example, I was once presented with a program that provided health care services to an urban, homeless population. At first glance, and from reading the program's literature, it seemed that appropriate evaluation criteria might involve considering the health status of the homeless. However, after getting to know the program, it became clear that the program's primary goal was to educate physicians and other health care workers about the plight of the homeless and the health ramifications of being homeless. Providing the homeless with on-the-spot medical treatment was a tool used to achieve the outcome that health care professionals would become more empathetic to treating the homeless.

Without a developed blueprint for the evaluation, there is a risk that the evaluation activities will continue ad infinitum. Separating the evaluation activities into seven discrete "tasks" allows evaluators to pause and to think about the direction that their activities should take.

The remainder of this book is devoted to more fully explaining each of these seven steps. By the end of the book, you should be able to carry out many evaluation activities independently. However, if you are faced with a particularly complex challenge that you cannot evaluate on your own, this book will have helped you develop enough expertise to become "educated consumers" of evaluation consultants, and you will be able to determine which consultants are most likely to carry out successful evaluation activities.

The remainder of this book is organized as follows. The first half focuses on developing the appropriate background for evaluation, and the second half addresses the use of quasi-experimentation in an evaluation context. Unlike many evaluation texts, this one emphasizes that one must rigorously describe the program prior to evaluation.

Chapter Two introduces the program logic model and program theory as tools to use when describing the program. The chapter closes with examples of program logic models and program theories from various types of programs, hoping to make you comfortable enough with these tools so that you will be able to apply them to one of your own programs.

Chapter Three discusses the framing of evaluation questions, elaborating upon the pre-evaluation steps that a good evaluator will complete.

Because all programs exist to cause change in the trajectory of those whom they serve, it is necessary to consider what "cause" means. Chapter Four delves into the meaning of causation in an evaluation context.

Chapter Five explicates "validity" and what it means to do valid evaluation research. Chapter Six introduces the reader to the quasi-experimental designs used, and how trade-offs are made between quasi-experimental designs and types of validity. Quasi-experimental design is used to attribute changes to a program.

Chapter Seven presents issues that arise when collecting data and when designing surveys, and considers sampling approaches. While the chapter does not substitute for a good course in statistics, it does discuss some of the more pertinent points.

Chapter Eight concludes the text, discussing the similarities between grant proposals and evaluation plans, both of which are essential to a good proposal.

SUMMARY

The primary job of the evaluator is to examine the impact of program interventions. A secondary job is to provide a critical perspective to improve programs. The goal of evaluation is to assist with continuous program improvement and introspection. To successfully evaluate a program, the evaluator must follow the steps of the evaluation framework.

KEY TERMS

evaluation	program theory
evaluators	quasi-experimental design
formative evaluations	summative evaluations
program logic model	target population

DISCUSSION QUESTIONS

1. What are the goals of program evaluation?

2. Why is it important to have an evaluation plan?

3. What is the evaluation framework?

CHAPTER

2

DESCRIBING THE PROGRAM

LEARNING OBJECTIVES

After reading this chapter, you should be able to

- Explain the importance of involving stakeholders
- Describe program theory
- Describe the program logic model (PLM)
- List common mistakes evaluators make when describing a program

Before beginning an evaluation of a program, an evaluator first needs to develop a thorough understanding of the program. This understanding must be shared by the program's stakeholders; if the evaluator's understanding is different, the stakeholders will not use the evaluation results because their program will be unrecognizable to them. The program's stakeholders typically include any or all of the following groups:

- Program administrator(s)

- Program funders

- The board of directors of the organization offering the program

- Program clients

- Program staff

- Advocates for the program

- Potential recipients of the program's services

- Alumni of the program

Each set of stakeholders' different perspectives on the program must be understood and included in order to develop a well-rounded description of the program.

Evaluators use two graphical tools to rigorously describe a program: **program theory,** which is a diagram of the theory behind the program as perceived by the program's personnel; and the **program logic model,** which models the operation of the program and the logic behind the program.

These two models each consider the program in an interrelated but different light. The program theory, representing the program's "theory of change," describes the theoretical chain of which the program believes it is a part. In contrast, the program logic model details the program's operations, its available resources, its target population, and its goals.

When the program theory and program logic model both reflect the reality of the program, the program benefits. With appropriate modeling, you can clearly see opportunities for program improvement and concise ways to evaluate the program's processes and outcomes. Rarely does a program not appear in need of some improvement when articulated through these three approaches.

If time and effort are expended on developing an accurate program description, then the opportunities for evaluation and the evaluation questions become obvious. Developing a thorough understanding of the program allows you to create the most parsimonious evaluation approach. Evaluators like the word "parsimony"—it comes up often in evaluation. By definition, it means "unusual or excessive frugality; extreme economy or stinginess." In evaluation, "parsimonious" describes the smallest set of questions that will deliver the most bang for the buck. Before starting on an evaluation, the evaluation questions should be whittled down to the most "parsimonious" set. Very poorly planned evaluation studies—such as those that use a ridiculous number of outcome measures, thinking that at least one of them will reflect the result of the program—occur when a thorough understanding of the program has not been developed.

Parsimonious program models clarify which evaluatory outcome measures to use, thus allowing you to ultimately collect and analyze smaller amounts of data, saving time (and money) in the data collection and analysis stages.

MOTIVATIONS FOR DESCRIBING THE PROGRAM

Other interrelated motivations behind the development of a program's program theory and program logic model are that by creating these models, the program increases both the probability of success and attracting money.

Once the program has been rigorously and parsimoniously described in a way that reflects how program personnel see it, and there is consensus around the program theory and program logic model, program personnel will use the description to attract support and clients. Funders today want to support well-articulated programs with clear and concise goals. They want to fund programs that program personnel have thought through. Nothing establishes the credibility of a program more than showing that the organization in which the program is housed has carefully thought through every aspect of the program.

Although funders may require a program description in formats other than a program logic model and program theory, having these descriptions on paper allows for ready adaptation to the format needed for any grant proposal. Thus, the organization's development personnel should become familiar with the interpretation of the program logic model and program theory.

Conversely, nothing will make funders question the credibility of a program or organization more than if they feel that they have to do the thinking behind the program. If a funder has reason to question the program's underlying theory, then it is likely that funder will not support it. Further, if the funder is the one who brings to the attention of others possible unintended negative consequences of the program, then the credibility of the organization and program will also be questioned.

Yet another motivation to develop a thorough program description is that it can be shared with current and potential clients of the program, assuring that all staff share the same vision of the program with current and potential clients. A well-articulated program is more likely to attract appropriate clients. When programs are "fuzzy" in their description, they are more likely to attract clients for whom the program is inappropriate. When programs are clear and concise in their descriptions, potential clients are better able to decide whether the services offered are a good fit for their situation.

In terms of public relations, this shared vision means that potential clients, program staff, and other stakeholders all receive and transmit a consistent, clear message about the program's goals and activities. Staff will be unified in setting priorities and determining which aspects of their activities to emphasize, thus decreasing the chances that staff will go astray and that services offered will differ between program personnel.

Common Mistakes Evaluators Make When Describing the Program

One of the most common mistakes evaluators make is to rush through developing a thorough understanding of the program. The following reasons account for this error:

■ The evaluator imposes on the program his or her interpretation of how the program *should* operate or *is* operating.

■ The evaluator and stakeholders are so focused on "outcome measures" that they feel they do not have time to develop an appropriate understanding of the program. That is, evaluation is misinterpreted as an exercise in producing or explaining outcome measures.

■ The evaluator has relied on a small number of stakeholders for program knowledge, and the stakeholders themselves may not have a good understanding of the program. This might be the case when relying only on administrators and board members rather than on-the-ground staff.

■ It may be in the best interests of the few stakeholders to present the program in as favorable a light as possible.

■ The evaluator relies only on written materials about the program to develop an understanding of it. When relying on grant proposals, you should be aware that grant proposals are written to attract money, and a disconnect can exist between what was promised to attract funds and how the program actually works or on what the program focuses. Evaluators should also be wary of many aspects of annual reports, which are often used for development purposes and thus tend to show the program in the most favorable light, again yielding a potential disconnect between the program's image and reality.

Developing a shared understanding of the program takes time. Because it is the evaluator's understanding of the program that determines exactly what will be evaluated, it is essential that the evaluator's understanding be precisely on target and that everybody invest in this critical evaluation stage.

Conducting the Initial Informal Interviews

The best way for the evaluator to start building an understanding of the program is for the evaluator to conduct informal interviews with a number of stakeholders. In these interviews, which can be one-on-one or between the evaluator and a group of stakeholders no larger than a focus group (approximately eight people), the evaluator asks about the goals of the program, how the program is implemented, and goes on-site to observe the program. Typical questions that may be asked in the informal interviews include the following:

- What events or circumstances led to the program's creation?

- Who thought of the program?

- How was the perceived need for the program determined?

- Is the program modeled on other programs? If so, which ones?

- Why did the program's creators think that it would work in this location at this time?

- From where does funding for the program come?

- How does the program sustain itself?

- How much does it cost to run the program? How have the costs changed over time? Are there any in-kind contributions that defray costs of the program?

- How does the current program differ from the original plan for the program?

- How large and dire is the need for the program?

- What proportion of those in need does the program serve?

- How are staff recruited?

- Are there issues with staff retention?

- What sort of training do staff go through?

- What processes exist to assure that staff adhere to the program's design?

- What do clients expect from the program?

- Do clients stick with the program? Why or why not?

- Are there any apparent unintended effects (positive or negative) of the program?

- Does the program have critics? Who are they? What do they say about the program?

Pitfalls in Describing Programs

Common pitfalls in describing programs include situations where evaluators put on paper only what **reflects the program in its best light**. This results in a description not of the program as it actually exists, but of a program examined through rose-colored glasses. This can be compared to someone's hiring a personal trainer without revealing how out of shape he actually is. The trainer cannot develop an appropriate plan to get the person in shape.

Another pitfall is to **use only the input of the "higher ups."** This can also result in the description of a fantasy program. The people on the ground—those directly interacting with clients, making personnel decisions, and procuring resources for the program—will not share this understanding of the program, and thus ultimately will not recognize the program evaluated.

A third pitfall occurs when **the evaluator takes control of the program description.** Here, an evaluator has completed the models for the program and has done the work for the program rather than working with the program in creating the program description. This is a subtle but important difference. Nothing should be included or excluded from the models without the program personnel's full knowledge and agreement. Although this may produce a model of an infeasible program, the iterative process itself will produce a learning opportunity for the program. If the evaluator does the work for the client, then the evaluator has robbed the program personnel of the opportunity to learn and to better understand their own program. Further, if the evaluator takes too much control of the evaluation process, then the program personnel will never buy in to the evaluation or evaluatory activities and thus will never be fully vested in the results of the evaluation.

It can be tempting for the evaluator to take control of the program description, especially if the evaluator has gone through the process with seemingly similar programs and if the stakeholders do not have a consistent view of the program. A program description may stall because of differing stakeholders' views. It may seem that time is being wasted because the stakeholders differ on what ought to be included in the description tools. However, a wise evaluator will allow the stakeholders to work it out by incorporating all of their views, giving them an opportunity to delete from the models what seems irrelevant. The program's stakeholders then have the opportunity to create a shared vision of the program.

I cannot stress enough that a program will become more effective, focused, and successful when all of the program's stakeholders share a detailed understanding of the program and reach a consensus on the logic model and theory. Even subtle discrepancies in the various parties' views of the program can diffuse the program's effectiveness. Once stakeholders share an understanding of the program, it can become more focused. Generally, the more focused a program is, the greater the likelihood that the program will be successful in reaching its goals. Thus, the evaluator can act as a mediator between stakeholders, but should never take control of the models.

THE PROGRAM IS ALIVE, AND SO IS ITS DESCRIPTION

Evaluators should think of the models that result as living documents that perpetually grow and change. How you have described a program at one time may not be valid at another time. Because of the fluidity of the environments in which most programs operate, the descriptive models of a program should be periodically revisited (such as every three to six months) to assure that they still apply to the program as it exists at a particular time.

For this reason, it is vital that all program descriptions be dated, allowing you to examine the program's evolution over time, as well as providing a history of the program. I have noticed that most nonprofits do not have a document that describes a program's history. Such a document enables the organization to keep track of when decisions about the program were made, when changes were implemented, and who was administering the program at the time. Understanding the program's history allows you to better understand the program's current form. Frequently, though, when asking about the program's history, many nonprofits have trouble recounting it—they look for guidance from personnel who may have been with the program over the years. Having the program description dated and retained allows one to see how the program operated in the past, under what assumptions, and under what theory. Keeping track of the program's history can help the program from reverting back to practices that it had abandoned for good reason.

Comparing the current program against past descriptions provides an opportunity to ask questions about why the program has morphed into its current incarnation. There should be good reasons for changes. Programs can go astray from their original design because they want to take advantage of perceived opportunities (for example, funding opportunities that may exist if the program did something a little differently, such as reaching a new target population, or offering a slightly altered service). Although taking advantage of such opportunities may seem beneficial in the short term, there is the risk that the program could become something that was never intended.

Some programs add on new "components," either in the short term or for the long term. Adding some components may be appropriate, but evaluators should check the degree to which the added components make the program deviate from its intended goals and activities, and whether the stakeholders are actually comfortable with the deviation, once it is pointed out to them via the program description tools.

Stakeholders should be conscious of the reasons why and in which respects a program has changed. Sometimes, programs change because they have matured and developed a better sense of what works and what doesn't. In this sense, we can see that the program is on the same growth trajectory as originally intended. Sometimes, though, programs deviate from their intended path and enter a different trajectory. Left unchecked, they may begin a different orbit, becoming unrecognizable to the program planners. This change may be appropriate, but shouldn't be undertaken without deep consideration.

There is no clear place to start when modeling a program. I start with the program theory because my personal approach tends to be theoretical. Other practitioners may feel more comfortable starting with the program logic model. The development of both approaches—program theory and program logic model—is iterative, meaning that the evaluator and stakeholders should go back and forth on these models as many times as it takes to assure that the results reflect reality, before moving on to measurement.

Program Theory

The program theory should reflect the "if" statements that are relevant to the program. The "if" statements are similar to the following:

> *If we do A, then B will happen, then C will happen, then . . . and finally we will observe a change in Y.*

In addition to the general reasons articulated in the previous section, modeling the program theory is an important and necessary step because it allows the program to articulate its vision of how and through which mechanisms the program anticipates change resulting from its activities. Every program exists because it believes that it causes change, but getting the program to display how short-term and (perhaps) long-term change will result from its activities reveals the realm in which the program operates. By revealing the chain of the causal process, the program theory potentially reveals weaknesses in connections between the program's activities and anticipated outcomes.

Getting everybody on board about the program's theoretical underpinnings has value in that it helps stakeholders, and especially program staff, to reflect on exactly what the program theoretically aims to accomplish. Having this explicitly articulated directs staff on how they should consider the services they provide.

Diagramming the Program Theory Creating an appropriate diagram of the program theory is more an art than a science, and can be the most challenging part of developing the evaluation plan. Sometimes, knowing where to begin is not clear, but this ultimately should not matter, because developing the program theory is an iterative process that works best when the evaluator asks prompting questions during the informal interviews, revealing the program's theoretical assumptions.

Discussions with program stakeholders provide the first draft of the program theory. The draft is shared with the stakeholders for their review, with the evaluator's facilitation. This process continues until all agree on a satisfactory program theory.

Further, the program theory distinguishes the program's short-term from its long-term goals and reveals the programmatic goals that may exist at different units of analysis.

In drafting the program theory, I find it easiest to start with the program's activities, first considering possible short-term changes, and then long-term changes. Finally, I get the organization to "fill in" the causal chain, by asking what seem like naïve questions, such as "How does B cause C?" Sometimes, because personnel have been a part of the program for so long and have bought into its ideals, they haven't delineated the exact process through which change might occur. Sometimes, when personnel discuss what they expect from an intervention, they gloss over the intermediate steps either because they haven't considered them for some time, or have never really thought through the causal chain in any amount of detail. These intermediate steps are important to articulate because they directly relate to the program's probable success in producing the desired changes. The simplest questions can reveal the biggest assumptions that the program makes.

Another aspect of the program theory is the **unit of analysis** of the changes. The unit of analysis is the "thing" that is of interest. Some programs operate at many units of analysis. For example, a program may have individuals as clients, but aim to affect families, households, neighborhoods, and municipalities. All of these represent different units of analysis. Some programs serve children, but also want to affect classrooms, teachers, schools, and curriculum. I knew of one program that worked with individual doctors, but hoped to affect hospitals and even the entire health care system. One can examine the program's theory of change at each unit of analysis, or the unit of analysis can be built into a single program theory. For some programs that operate at many different levels, it may make sense to create more than one program theory, reflecting the different realms in which the program operates.

When considering the issue of the unit of analysis, be wary of incorrectly thinking that the unit of analysis must get broader the further you go down the causal chain. This is not the case. I have seen programs that interact with individuals but aim to affect communities, and I have seen other programs that interact with communities but aim to ultimately affect individuals. Sometimes those who are novices at creating a program theory incorrectly think that they must start with individuals and then broaden the program's effects to families, communities, and then, even broader.

There is a fine line between having a causal chain that is detailed enough and having one that is too detailed to be useful. Later in this chapter, in Example 1, an international union's training programs illustrates this issue.

Even if the program theory that stakeholders articulate seems weak to the evaluator, displaying a weak program theory has merit, in that it exposes flaws in the program's design.

It is common for the first drafts of a program's theory to look somewhat like a plate of spaghetti, with abundant linkages between levels of analysis (for example, leading from individuals to the community level), lines showing subprocesses, a multitude of short-term and long-term effects, and myriad units of analysis. The program theory usually becomes cleaner when, upon introspection, stakeholders reconsider their original ideas.

It is the evaluator's responsibility to display the program theory in the leanest way possible, creating a program theory that has no lines that cross. The use of colors is an effective way to show different units of analysis. The diagram of the program theory should be detailed enough to reveal the steps in the causal chain, but not so detailed that at first glance it seems overwhelming and unintelligible. Words and expressions in the program theory should take on their common meaning rather than some special meaning that only program personnel or people with specific knowledge would use.

Probably the best way to learn how to construct a program theory diagram is to examine some that have already been created. I start with one of my favorite programs, the Opera Trunk Program. I include this on my list of favorites because it is focused, its objectives are clear, and its logic suggests that it has a chance of success.

This program is what many might consider a "small" program. It does not aim to change the world; its only goal is to sustain opera in society by creating an interest in opera among schoolchildren. In this program, a city's opera company created elaborately decorated trunks and filled them with materials associated with an opera. These trunks would travel to various elementary classrooms in the region and be used to introduce children to a particular opera. The outside of the trunk was decorated to reflect the opera (for example, the trunk for *Madame Butterfly* had a Japanese motif),

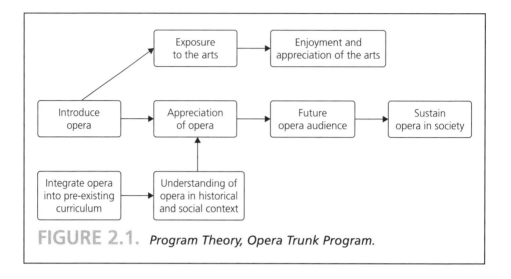

FIGURE 2.1. *Program Theory, Opera Trunk Program.*

and contained various paraphernalia related to the opera—a recording, costumes, materials on the history of the opera's locale, and other meaningful items. In addition to using the trunk, local elementary teachers were invited to participate in a one-day workshop on introducing opera to children and how to integrate opera into existing curricula. The workshop was held on a Saturday, and teachers were not given a stipend for their attendance.

The Opera Trunk Program's program theory (Figure 2.1) suggests that its stakeholders felt that if children were introduced to opera, then they would develop an increased appreciation of opera, which would in the future increase the audience for opera, ultimately enhancing opera's sustainability.

In this case, the program also would have positive "spillover" effects onto other art forms. The introduction of opera increases exposure to the arts, thus enhancing children's enjoyment and appreciation of the arts in general, a positive end in and of itself. Although sustaining opera was the chief intent, noting the positive spillover effect in the program theory helped build the case for the program.

Another causal chain activated by this program occurs through the integration of opera into the teachers' curricula. This was thought to lead to an increase of children's understanding of opera in the historical and social context in which the opera was written. A greater understanding of the context of the opera was thought to increase children's appreciation of opera, which again, would ultimately sustain opera in society.

Many arts education programs follow a similar program theory, where the end goal is both appreciation of the specific art form and appreciation of the arts in general. Additionally, many children's arts education programs go beyond art appreciation to teaching how to create art. When creation is part of the program, then the program theory would likely have the additional goal of inspiring more artists, both on a professional and amateur basis.

Program Theory and Literature Reviews By explicating the program theory in a diagram, anyone could readily see how the program's designers expect the program to produce positive results. An important side-product of detailing the program's theory is that it helps determine which literature one should review to provide evidence of links in the causal chain. Long ago, an advisor told me to "read with a purpose." With the program theory in hand, one purpose of the literature review becomes revealing whether the program theory is sound and reasonable.

Literature usually exists on some or all aspects of the program theory, and the evaluator should review the literature on each of the connections made in the program theory. For example, if A causes B and B causes C and . . . F causes G, then the literature reviewed should determine the foundation for and veracity of each of these statements.

In the Opera Trunk Program, according to the program theory, the literature review should try to answer the following questions: Does introducing opera to schoolchildren increase their appreciation of opera? To what extent does the appreciation of opera while young create a willingness to attend opera in the future? Does integration of opera into the curriculum increase children's understanding of the opera's historical and social context? Does this increased understanding lead to an appreciation of opera? Does exposure to any art form increase the enjoyment and appreciation of other arts? Does developing a future opera audience result in sustaining opera in society?

Using Program Theory to Narrow the Evaluation Questions The program theory and the corresponding literature review reveal which links in the causal chain are virtually certain to occur and which are more tenuous. The links in the program theory virtually certain to occur are aspects where one would devote few, if any, evaluation resources beyond the literature review. Evaluation resources should be devoted to exploring such tenuous links as these are the areas where the program's theory may be vulnerable. For example, if I know with certainty that if C occurs D will result, then in deciding upon the areas to evaluate I do not need to reinvent the wheel and show the C–D linkage, as the existing literature will support this certainty.

The literature review may reveal that the connection between C and D is very strong but that the connection between B and C is more uncertain. Depending on the strength of the theoretical relationship, this may indicate that you need not bother showing that C affects D but instead can focus possibly scarce evaluation resources on examining the B–C link.

In the Opera Trunk Program, some of the linkages are more uncertain than others. For example, the degree to which introducing opera to children results in enhanced appreciation of opera is probably uncertain. However, the link between future opera audiences and the sustenance of opera is so strong that it can be taken off the list of possible questions, as it falls into the category of linkages that are so strong that re-examining them would be equivalent to reinventing the wheel. Thus, the literature, rather than primary data collection, can be relied upon to prove linkages.

The program theory also clarifies which linkages will be seen in the short term rather than long term. Programs that are offered only on a short time frame cannot examine long-term impacts. To make the case for a long-term impact, the program must turn to the literature. Ideally, the literature can be relied upon to make the case that if the short-term impact occurs, the long-term effects will be eventually seen.

The Program Logic Model

Another way of examining a program is through a program logic model, which intends to examine the following questions:

- Does the program have the resources it needs to operate?

- Is the program intense enough to produce the intended outcomes?

- Are the program's goals and outcomes feasible?

- Are the program's assumptions about the environment in which it operates realistic?

- Is the program's reliance on resources realistic? Will the resources it needs to operate be there on a continuous basis?

- Is the program's target population well-specified and within reach?

Similar to the program theory, the program logic model reveals the program under a harsh light. It does not address the theoretical underpinnings of the program, focusing instead on the operation of the program.

The version of the program logic model that I use and advocate is presented in Table 2.1. It is an adaptation of the W. K. Kellogg Foundation's (1998, 2001) program logic model. The power of the program logic model is not evident until all of the columns are completed for a program. Its power becomes apparent when you step back from the program and critically think about its logic, the possible weaknesses, how it could be more focused, and the probability of success. Further, a tight logic model will reveal on which basis (outcomes or processes) the program should be evaluated.

Columns of the Program Logic Model The program logic model (PLM) has eight columns that must be completed: Goals, Assumptions, Target Population, Inputs, Activities, Outputs, Outcomes, and Outcome Measures.

The columns should be completed independently of each other. You should not create rows in the PLM. Some novices incorrectly create rows, start with a goal, and then try to complete each of the columns for a particular goal. Such an approach does not take a holistic view of the program and inevitably leads to some repetition (for example, the target population might be repeated for each goal). Instead, one should complete one column of the PLM and then move to the next. In this section, I will review each column and then present examples of completed program logic models.

TABLE 2.1. Program Logic Model (Theoretical).

Goals	Assumptions	Target Population	Inputs and Resources	Activities	Outputs	Outcomes	Outcome Measures
What the program intends to change or influence, which may include a primary goal and secondary goals, and both long-term and short-term goals	Assumptions upon which the program and its operation are based, usually phrased as statements about the program's environment or human behavior as perceived prior to the implementation of the program	Exactly whom the program is trying to change, usually bound by geography or population characteristics—a program never attempts to change everyone	The money, items, people, and in-kind contributions the program uses to operate—what it takes to run the program	What the program needs to do to engage participants and how it engages participants	Indicators of the program's operation	Aspects of the change that the program may have caused; operation-alizations of the goals	Mathematical measures of the outcomes

Goals. The goals column should reflect the change(s) that the program anticipates will result from its activities. The goals of the program should relate to the program theory. Usually, the program theory's ultimate goal, which is listed on the right-hand side of the program theory, is listed in the goals column of the PLM.

Often, programs have both long-term and short-term goals. For example, a program may have the short-term goal of providing foster children with stable and secure housing situations, with the ultimate goal that foster children will grow into well-adjusted, productive adults. In this case, the short-term goal in the PLM is an interim goal reflected in the program theory.

Programs may also have primary goals, or goals that the program must achieve, and secondary goals that are not the chief reason for the program's existence. For example, a program intended to spur the creation of green grocers in an inner city may have a primary goal of increasing access to fresh produce for people in isolated neighborhoods, but a secondary goal may be giving farmers direct access to consumers.

Working with organizations, I have found a pattern in developing the goals column of the program logic models. When a PLM is first developed, many program administrators seem to want the goals column to be as long as possible and list a multitude of goals. Often, these goals are broader than the program's actual activities; thus, if one were to evaluate the program based on these broad goals, it would surely seem unsuccessful.

The reason for the long list of goals may have to do with how organizations have historically applied for funding. Program administrators were sometimes given the impression that their funding application would have a higher likelihood of success if they stressed the larger possible set of outcomes of their programs, possibly overstating the possible impact of the program's activities. Administrators become tied to the goals articulated in funding applications. Thus, when an evaluator interviews personnel for the program logic model, the personnel still think in terms of a grant proposal.

Although I may question some of the goals and ask for clarification on how the program's activities could lead to those goals, I will keep the multitude of articulated goals in the first draft of the program logic model. When I later ask program personnel to review the PLM with me, I often find that they are willing to remove some of the goals listed in the first iteration of the PLM.

Conversely, I have seen programs list goals that they believe are somewhat peripheral to the main emphasis of the program—but once the entire program is fully described, it turns out that the peripheral goals are central to the program.

For these reasons, I advise that the first iteration of the PLM include all of the goals articulated by stakeholders. Developing the PLM is an iterative process, and it often takes much discussion between the evaluator and program personnel before an appropriate and concise PLM is created. Later drafts of the PLM will offer the opportunity to streamline goals and organize them into long-term versus short-term, and essential versus peripheral.

The worst mistake an evaluator can make in the PLM is to describe a program that the program's personnel do not recognize. Personnel ultimately must feel ownership of the product, and for this reason it is important that the first draft include all of the goals they articulated. This will help them to buy into the evaluation plan and evaluation activities.

Assumptions. The assumptions column ought to reflect how the program views the environment in which it operates. Some of these assumptions are valid and others have been proven true by collected data.

Still others, though, are not based on data, but solely on how program creators perceive the program's environment. Or, sometimes the assumptions reflect what was known about another place, population, or time, and bear no relation to the program's actual current circumstances or demographics.

Every program makes assumptions, but these assumptions are often not articulated. Articulating the assumptions is useful because it helps one to see whether the program is realistic or unrealistic about its environment.

Sometimes, the assumptions are negative goal statements. For example, if a program aims to decrease obesity in children by advocating for nutritious foods in schools, then the program is essentially assuming that children are obese because of a lack of nutritional content in school meals. Such a program also assumes that the nutritional content of foods in schools needs to be changed. The program may also be assuming that contractual agreements between school districts and their food providers allow for healthier food options and ultimately, that children will eat the nutritious foods. All of these are "big" assumptions, and the violation of any one of them could jeopardize the effectiveness of the program.

I have seen that when programs are colossal failures, they fail because of faulty assumptions. For example, a foundation-sponsored $80 million child-care program targeted at low-income communities failed because it made the following faulty assumptions:

(a) Low-income communities have a supply of buildings that one could inexpensively adapt for child-care uses

(b) Children in the participating low-income communities would only need part-time care, not full-time care

(c) There would be a supply of trained child-care professionals willing to work for the wages that child-care occupations offer

All of these assumptions are "big" assumptions that threatened the program's chances for success.

Other types of assumptions pertain to the program's inputs (that funding for the program will continue), program's staff (that trained personnel are available), and program's clients (that people desire the services the program offers). Sometimes, programs assume a shared perspective. All programs assume that their efforts are sufficient and intense enough to start a chain of events.

It is best to think through all of the possible assumptions that a program has made. Once these are listed, then the evaluator has the job of investigating how realistic the assumptions are. If any one assumption that the program has made is off base, the foundation of the program could be jeopardized and the program could fail.

Target Population. All programs "target" their efforts at a particular population. When one considers the target population, one should be thinking in terms of the "unit of analysis" that the program attempts to influence. The smallest unit of analysis is the individual level. Programs can target a more aggregated unit, such as families, households, neighborhoods, communities, or systems. A program can target one unit in hopes that other units will change. For example, a program may work directly with mothers in the hope that opportunities for their children and family will improve. One should think clearly about which unit of analysis the program directly targets, and which unit of analysis the program ultimately hopes to influence. Often, these units are the same, but they need not be.

Often, programs think that they are targeting "everybody" or perhaps every person who lives in a certain geographic zone. A target population such as this can usually be better specified. Very few programs actually target everybody in the same way. For example, I once worked with a program that trucked in fresh produce weekly to sell in low-income neighborhoods that lacked local grocers. At first, the program claimed that it targeted everybody in the neighborhoods. But after reflection, the program appropriately decided that it targeted the people who purchased food in each household. Another target for the program was people who received farmers' market coupons through the WIC program.

Often, the target population can be described demographically, and the size of the population can be estimated by using census data. In the United States, one can obtain population estimates for the country, states, counties, municipalities, census tracks (usually about three thousand people), and blocks from data collected in the most recent census, which is conducted at the beginning of each decade. The U.S. Census Bureau has the information available on its Web site (www.census.gov). A program should consider how well the program population—the population that avails itself to the program—reflects the target population.

Inputs. This column reveals what it takes to operate the program and should explicitly list the following: monetary funding; in-kind contributions; physical space; characteristics and qualifications of staff; particular expertise of staff; and sometimes the voluntary participation and assistance of others.

Listing the inputs to the program has three advantages. First, it allows one to objectively consider whether the program has enough resources to operate effectively. Listing the funding, as well as a summary of what the funding bought in terms of personnel and space, quickly gives an idea of the program's capacity.

Second, listing the inputs allows people who are considering replicating the program to observe what it takes to operate such a program. If the program used something special that was unique to a particular program and could not easily be replicated, then that should be listed. For example, if the program relies on the media, and someone on the board was able to secure scarce media time on a particular radio station, then that unique "connection" should be listed. Sometimes, programs may have charismatic leaders, or leaders who are extraordinarily competent or unique. Such leaders should be listed as inputs, since they will be difficult, if not impossible to replicate.

Third, listing the inputs provides the information that would be needed to do a cost-benefit analysis. In my opinion, you should delay doing an actual cost-benefit analysis until you have determined whether the program has any benefits. But a cost-benefit analysis can be useful in the hypothetical realm; you can ask the question "If the program were as successful as it could possibly be, what would be the cost per unit engaged in the program?" This analysis, though, has limited use other than providing a cost per minimum benefit received.

Another challenge with cost-benefit analysis is the difficulty of quantifying benefits. Some programs have spin-off and long-term benefits, and quantifying these benefits can be an inexact science. That is, for how many generations does one consider the benefits of a program that positively changes the earnings trajectory and life course of a participant? If a program directly influences one person who then becomes a community leader and develops a wider sphere of positive influence, how does one quantify that benefit? If a program increases one's likelihood of graduating from high school or college, should one only consider the difference in the participants' earnings or should one also consider effects on disease rates, mortality rates, and on the educational attainment of subsequent generations?

Sometimes, cost-benefit analyses can be molded to fit particular pre-conceived ideas. How to quantify the benefits becomes unclear, as do the true costs of the program. Should one consider opportunity costs of participants as costs?

For these reasons, I discourage cost-benefit analyses, but encourage rigorous examination of the benefits and the true costs of a program.

Activities. This column should briefly list what the program actually does, including the activities that the public may witness as well as the activities that go on behind the scenes. The activities listed in the PLM may be identical to those listed in a program implementation model, but the PLM may not go into as much detail. The activities column often includes how clients are recruited, how staff are trained, how the program reaches the target population, and how the program interacts with its clients.

Outputs. This column should reflect measures that the evaluator would take to show that the program is actually operating. Outputs include figures such as the number of clients. Outputs do not reflect any change, and they do not reflect whether a goal has been achieved.

I once worked with an intergenerational program, where the idea of the program was to get teenagers together with the elderly to produce visual artwork, and the teamwork would allow them to develop a better understanding of the challenges that the other generation faces. In that program, the number of visual art pieces would be an output. However, the change in the intergenerational understanding would be an outcome.

You may construct the outputs so that there is an output reflecting each step of the program's processes. Thinking about outputs in this way will reveal whether there are any "kinks" in the program's delivery of services or activities.

There are certain programs where the outputs may be the program's outcomes. In advocacy programs, the ultimate goal is usually to change the targeted population's stance on an issue. In reality, in political advocacy programs, there may be many reasons why politicians vote a particular way on an issue, and many of the reasons may be outside of the control of the advocacy organization. Holding the organization up to the standard of a changed vote on an issue might be too high (or too low) of a standard, depending on how public opinion on an issue may have shifted. In such situations, I recommend using the outputs as the program's outcomes, because actually being able to reach and inform about an issue may be as much as the organization can accomplish.

Outcomes. This column should reflect in words but not numbers the desired impact of the program; you need not be concerned about measurement issues when articulating outcomes. Your focus should be on what would have to change in order for the program to be considered successful. Similar to the goals column, the outcomes listed can be short-term or long-term outcomes, and include temporary effects of the program versus permanent effects. Usually, the outcomes relate to the program's goals and to intermediate steps in the program theory. Outcomes differ from goals in that they are usually operationalizations of the goals. When you "operationalize," you bring a theoretical concept down to the practical realm. For example, a goal of a program targeted to teenage foster children may be to have better prepared adults. The outcomes might include financial literacy, employment opportunities, functional romantic relationships, and so on.

Outcome Measures. This column should quantitatively reflect the measures, counts, rates, or indicators to use to operationalize the articulated outcomes.

There are a number of trade-offs to consider when committing to a quantitative outcome measure. First, consider whether the types of measures of the concept that are typically used are appropriate for the situation at hand. There are advantages to "borrowing" measures that are already prevalent. First, preexisting measures have usually been field tested to some degree. Second, using a preexisting measure allows comparisons between your program's outcomes and those of another program. The value of this cannot be overstated, because programs often want to make statements that suggest that they have been more effective than other programs that may compete for clients and funding. For these two important reasons, one should use preexisting outcome measures when appropriate.

However, sometimes the preexisting measures do not accurately apply to the program at hand, and in this case you need to create a new outcome measure—understanding that doing so will make the program incomparable with other programs because the different measures cannot be directly compared.

Any new outcome measure should have the following attributes. First, it should **exploit data that the program already collects, if possible**. When new data elements need to be collected for an outcome measure, then there is less likelihood that the new data will be collected right away. Even when there is a commitment to collecting the new information, it may take a while for the data collection system to run reliably and for the correct questions to be asked in order to collect the desired data.

Second, every outcome measure should have a **clearly defined unit of analysis.** The unit of analysis—the element to which the outcome measure applies—should be clear and explainable. One can readily interpret a unit of analysis of "child" given an age definition. However, the unit of analysis of "family" or "household" may need further explanation.

Third, all outcome measures should be **meaningful to stakeholders.** Stakeholders of the program should be able to readily understand why a particular measure is being used. If the best outcome measure, is very complex, but a close substitute is simple, then the program should opt for the simpler measure as it will be more transparent to stakeholders.

To save time and resources in the long run, I recommend developing a one-page sheet on each proposed outcome measure, which informs exactly how the measure is to work, starting with a discussion of how the measure is mathematically calculated. For example, is the measure a rate? If so, how are the numerator and denominator of the rate defined?

Second, describe exactly from where the data used in the measure are derived. Do the data come from the program's records? Is the number of residents in the community from census data?

Third, comment on the quality of the data that the measure uses. Are the data reliably kept? Are the data fraught with "measurement error"?

Fourth, describe whether any primary data collection is needed for the measure. Discuss why data that are already collected are insufficient for the program's purposes, describe measures used by similar programs, and explain why such measures are inappropriate for the program at hand.

The outcome measure sheets are internal documents intended to clarify the data collection needs of the evaluation process. However, they also give the organization a history of the measure, and in that sense, serve as a blueprint for calculating the measure, which ultimately will allow the measure to retain the same meaning over time. The exercise of developing an outcome sheet prevents the program from moving from outcome to outcome without very good reason. Creating such a sheet for each outcome measure may seem like a burdensome task, but this task actually will save you from making mistakes that could be costly in terms of time, money, and goodwill.

Stepping Back from the PLM Like the program theory, creating the program logic model is an iterative process, and the evaluator should consult with stakeholders to assure that the PLM appropriately reflects the program. The evaluator then reviews the program logic model, preferably with personnel from the program, to see how well, on paper, the program holds together. The essence of the PLM is that it allows one to creatively reflect on the program's chances of success, and how that success ought to be measured.

The evaluator, along with program stakeholders, should verify that the PLM's outcome measures relate to the goals. There should be no "orphans" in the program logic model—every goal is a candidate for measurement, every activity relates to at least one goal, and if a goal has no activities associated with it, then either the goal should be removed or activities should be developed. I usually choose removing goals over developing activities, because if the goal were truly important, the program would have already been engaged in related activities.

When reviewing the PLM, the evaluator should ask the following questions:

- How realistic are the program's assumptions?

- Is the target population well-specified and an achievable program population?

- To what degree does the program population reflect the target population?

- Does the program have the resources it needs to have the desired impact?

- Are the program's efforts intense enough to produce the desired impact?

- Do the goals of the program relate to the program outcomes?

- Do the outcome measures truly reflect the program's goals and outcomes?

- Does the program have enough resources to attract a well-trained staff?

The PLM shows the program in a very harsh light. Strong, focused programs usually shine under the spotlight of the PLM, but weaknesses in programs become painfully evident.

I once had the experience of working with three very different food assistance programs over a three-year period. Although the programs were run by three different organizations and had very different activities—a community gardens program, an advocacy effort, and a program that operated a produce truck for low-income, urban neighborhoods—they were bundled together in a grant because a pot of money was suddenly available. Each program approached the creation of the program logic model in the same way. At first, they all had very large goals. For example, the truck program believed that it was doing economic development. Each of the programs was committed to the big goals for about four to six months. As time went on, each of the programs dropped the goals that were tangential to the program and strengthened the activities and measures of the goals that were essential to the programs. That is, over time, each of the programs developed a "leaner and meaner" program logic model.

Programs with lean and mean PLMs often have a number of advantages over programs with extensive, broad PLMs. First, outsiders can easily see the program's logic; the program becomes transparent.

Second, program personnel can better define the boundaries of the program—articulating not only what the program is about, but just as importantly, what it is not about. Programs need limits, and the program logic model is a tool for demarcating these limits. The PLM thus helps the program to develop its own niche and to focus its services and activities there. Programs with broad PLMs have little opportunity for true success, because it is very difficult to be successful when resources and efforts are spread too thin.

Third, programs can check in with the PLM before undertaking new activities or changing the program's focus or activities. It is not unusual for programs to lose their focus. Some stakeholders may want to take advantage of dubious opportunities (for example, more funding may be available if the program changes in what seems like a minor way), or a program may decide to add on temporary components. Before modifying the program, personnel should check the PLM to see how the modification could affect the integrity of the program. Further, if an evaluation plan was based on a former version of the PLM, then any modification to the program may make the evaluation plan obsolete.

Challenges of Programs with Multiple Sites

Some programs operate at multiple sites; we will refer to a program site as a project. In describing multisite programs, one ought to consider whether on a day-to-day basis the projects actually should be considered the same program. Do they really share the same program theory and PLM? Do they really have the same emphasis? If a program has been designed to allow projects the flexibility to respond to local needs, have the projects responded to the same challenges in the same way, or is there so much "flexibility" that the sites should be considered separate and distinct programs?

One way of considering these questions is to develop individual program theories and PLMs for each project—these independent results can then be compared to determine the degree of consistency between projects.

Frequently, a program's projects have evolved in different ways. This could occur if the projects are able to take advantage of local conditions, respond to local needs, and draw their staff from local labor pools. Some programs encourage their projects to be responsive to local circumstances. When evaluating multisite programs, you need to first address the question of whether the projects actually represent the same program. For example, the Children's Health Insurance Program, a federal program, has different eligibility criteria across states and the benefits covered by the states can differ. The WIC program also offers different benefits in each state. When these programs are to be evaluated, one should question whether the differences between the states make a national evaluation useful. Instead, perhaps each state's program should be evaluated independently.

Simply documenting the similarities and differences between the projects can provide program directors with valuable information. If differences between the projects have evolved, the program's directors should be made aware of these differences. They may choose to bring all of the projects in line with the original design or, alternatively, to reconsider whether those that vary significantly ought to continue operating under the auspices of the program. In the extreme, having different projects operate under the same program title could dilute the integrity of the program.

PROGRAM IMPLEMENTATION MODEL

A final way to describe the program is through a program implementation model, which reflects a sequence of the program's activities and is akin to a flowchart. The model starts with the activities that the program sponsors, even before reaching the public, to the final stages, which may include analysis of a participant's data. That is, the model would describe how the program is staffed and marketed before moving on to the activities in which the program engages individuals.

The advantage of creating a program implementation model is that it allows you to clearly see opportunities for process-based evaluation. That is, collecting data on the various steps of the program can assure staff that both public and non-public activities are being carried out as intended. You can look for places where the workflow does not seem to be going smoothly. For example, you could ask such questions as:

- Are staff being hired as planned?

- Do staff members possess the qualifications that the program planners envisioned?

- Is the program being marketed properly?

- How much time does it take to process applications to the program?

- Are the services being delivered in a timely manner?

Simple flowcharts of the activities of a program can help pinpoint opportunities to improve the program as designed. However, flowcharts cannot help improve programs that have flawed designs or are based on faulty assumptions.

PROGRAM THEORY AND PROGRAM LOGIC MODEL EXAMPLES

The following examples present various frameworks to address a variety of evaluation challenges that programs present. These programs were selected because they demonstrate common issues that arise. The reader should understand the logic behind how the evaluation challenge was addressed, but also be aware that another approach to the evaluation challenge could have been taken.

EXAMPLE 1:   More Than One Program Described Under the Same Umbrella

An International Union, Local X, Training Programs

Figures 2.2 through 2.5 follow the evolution of the program theory for an initiative of a labor union that offers two types of training programs. These two "programs" are combined into one program theory model because the union thinks of the two of them as different aspects of the same effort. One program is an ongoing skills development program through which union members can take courses to improve or expand upon their existing skills. For example, a bulldozer operator can participate in the training to learn how to be a crane operator or to how to operate different types of bulldozers. The other type of skills training offered is an apprenticeship program, whereby people with no relevant skills go through training to learn how to be an operating engineer, and then apprentice on work sites over a four-year period at reduced pay.

The union is somewhat unique in that it is the conduit between employers and workers. Typically, employers will make requests to the union for workers who operate heavy equipment. Employers usually need union members for temporary employment—when construction or destruction is occurring.

To arrive at a good program theory of the training programs, the evaluator started with a bare framework. By providing training, the union believes that it will see increases in the certification of members, in skills diversification, and in apprenticeships. These improvements will in turn enhance members' qualifications, leading to increased member satisfaction, which will ultimately strengthen the union. This first draft of the program theory poorly specifies the theoretical pathway between (a) increased qualifications of union members and employer satisfaction and (b) employer satisfaction and strengthening of the union. The model needs work.

The second draft of the program theory makes more explicit the theoretical linkage between more highly qualified members and increased employer satisfaction. In this draft, the union theorized that if members are more highly qualified, the union will be able to fill a greater proportion of employer's requests for workers, which will increase employer satisfaction. And, if more employer requests are filled, the union will be strengthened. The second draft leaves open the question of how increased employer satisfaction leads to a strengthened union.

The third draft better specifies the linkage between increased employer satisfaction and a strengthened union by saying that if employers are more satisfied, then union members are more employable (or that employers are more likely to turn to the union than to non-union operating engineers when they have job openings). Increased employability means that union members will enjoy increased earnings and job satisfaction—and thus, will be more loyal to the union. Further, an increase in members' earnings allows the union to increase its dues. Having more resources and more loyal members strengthens the union.

The final version of the program theory clearly describes how diversity strengthens the union. The apprenticeship program, designed to increase the ethnic, racial, and age diversity of members, would theoretically allow the union to fulfill more employer requests, thus increasing employer satisfaction. Although not expressed in the program theory, in conversation union personnel reflected that if the union was more diverse, minorities would see it as a good alternative to being hired on a freelance or day-laborer basis. Decreasing competition leads to a strengthened union.

The final program theory is well explicated and adding any more to it might make it too complex. There is a fine line between a well-explicated program theory and one that is so complex that it is difficult for external audiences to comprehend. External audiences, including potential funders, often do not have the time or interest to decipher complex models of the program theory. This final program theory, in my opinion, successfully explains the complexity of the initiative in a clear, parsimonious way. One can readily understand the union's perspective on its training programs.

The program theory also helps the evaluator decide which literature to read to understand the program's chances of success. Literature on the following questions should be examined:

- What factors are associated with strong unions?
- Does increasing the pool of people with certifiable skills in a union cause employers to hire union versus non-union members? What other factors affect employers' hiring practices?

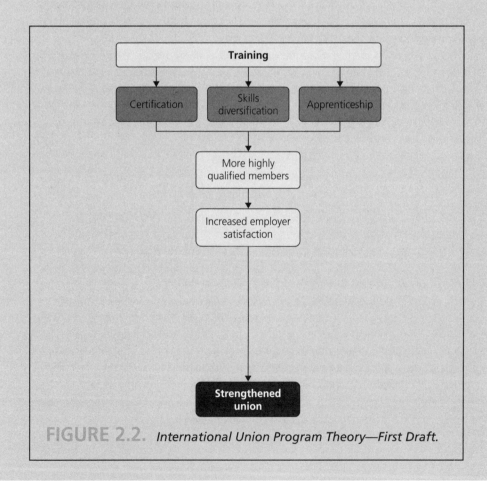

FIGURE 2.2. *International Union Program Theory—First Draft.*

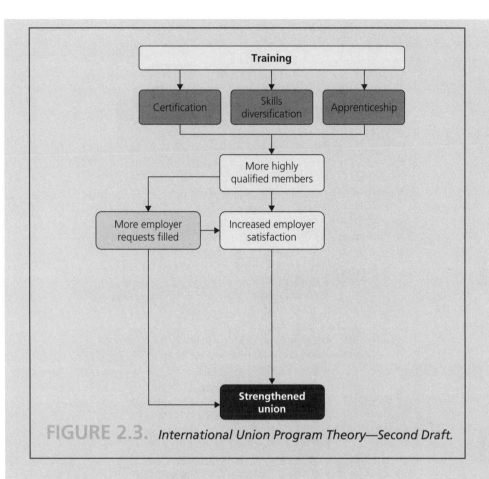

FIGURE 2.3. *International Union Program Theory—Second Draft.*

■ What threats to union strength exist?

■ What factors are associated with loyalty to one's union?

Reading the literature on all of these questions will help you to theorize whether the program can be successful in the ways that it wants to be. If the literature is extremely "tight," meaning that it has repeatedly shown that the program will have its intended impact when it is implemented properly and begins moving through the theoretical chain, it may be unnecessary to carry out evaluation activities beyond showing that the program is being implemented as intended. If the program is being implemented appropriately, the theoretical chain of events has been started, and the literature shows that the impacts are highly likely to occur, then evaluation activities should be restricted to the program implementation aspect.

It is important that the program theory also inform what literature should *not* be examined. In this case, literature on the following question should be avoided:

What is the effect of job training programs on the unemployed and underemployed?

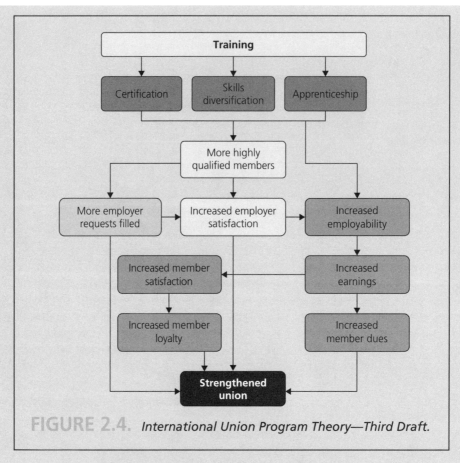

FIGURE 2.4. *International Union Program Theory—Third Draft.*

There is an enormous literature in the field of labor economics on this question, and before explicating the program theory, an evaluator may be tempted to put "job training" into a search engine, and would inevitably be overwhelmed by the sheer number of articles and books that would be found. However, by explicating the program theory, we could see that much of this literature would not be relevant to the union's specific programs. Having a program theory at hand before conducting a literature review ultimately saves time and resources.

THE PROGRAM LOGIC MODEL

The union's PLM for this initiative is shown in Table 2.2.

Because this program was intended to have an impact in different ways—from developing skills of current union members to establishing an apprentice program—the evaluators thought it best to separate out these aspects so they could better communicate the PLM to the union, which would further enable the union to better communicate with potential funders.

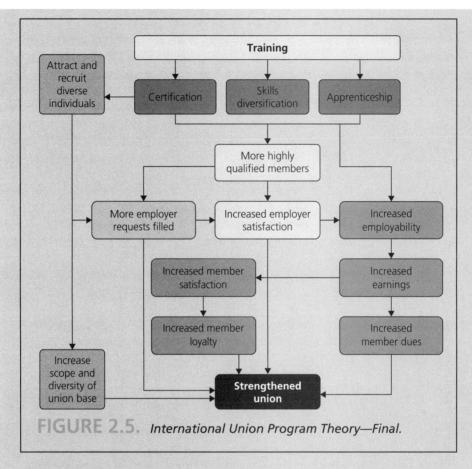

FIGURE 2.5. *International Union Program Theory—Final.*

The columns of this PLM are well specified. It is clear that if the assumptions of the program were violated, the integrity of the entire program would be at risk, greatly decreasing the program's likelihood of success. Some assumptions, for example, "Union members' well-being needs to be improved," seem well grounded. However, other assumptions—such as "Members want to enhance their skills" and "Skills training will meet employers' demand for workers"—should be supported with data, perhaps from a needs assessment. In this case, you would want to carry out needs assessments, which in this case would be a survey of union members to estimate the extent to which they want to enhance their skills and a survey of employers to determine which additional skills they would like union members to possess.

OUTLINE OF EVALUATION PLAN

Based on the PLM and program theory, you can start to outline what the evaluation plan for these training programs would look like. With respect to employers, consider both the total number of employer requests and the percentage of total requests that are

TABLE 2.2. Program Logic Model (International Union).

Goals	Assumptions	Target Population	Inputs	Activities	Outputs	Outcomes	Outcome Measures
<u>Union</u> Improve members' well-being Improve work conditions of all workers <u>Skills training</u> Increase members' employability (income, rates) Satisfy employer need for high-quality operating engineers Increase member loyalty and participation in the union	<u>Union</u> Members' well-being needs to be improved Unionization can improve well-being There is power in numbers High employer satisfaction strengthens union Member satisfaction increases loyalty <u>Skills training</u> Meets employers' demand for skilled union members	<u>Union</u> All operating engineers <u>Skills training</u> Current members Potential members <u>Apprentices</u> Age in early 20s High level of physical coordination High scores on aptitude tests	<u>Union</u> Funding from union dues <u>Skills training</u> Instructors Workshop equipment and material <u>Apprentices</u> Jobs and wages by employer Training and support from union Joint labor-management board	<u>Union</u> Administer benefits package Political advocacy Referral services for jobs Training <u>Skills training</u> Advertise classes Run seminars and workshops, conducted seasonally	<u>Skills training</u> Number of classes taught each year Number of students trained per skill area <u>Apprentices</u> Number of apprentices trained Number of apprentices who are active union members	<u>Skills training</u> Better-skilled union members with better chances of employment —higher skill level —higher skill diversification Increased employer requests filled Increased employer satisfaction	<u>Skills training</u> Employer evaluations Number of employer requests and number filled by the union Number of hours worked per member per year Mean number of union activities member is involved in Number of new union members enrolled in program <u>Apprentices</u> Apprentice and employer evaluations

Apprentices Increase diversity (minorities and women)	Members want to enhance their skills and need increased employment Apprentices Apprentices will not adversely affect employment opportunities for current members Apprentices are needed to replace retirees. The program will appeal to minorities	Solid education Satisfied with a medium- to low-level income Individuals from diverse backgrounds, particularly minorities and women	Issuing certifications or licenses Apprentices 6-week pre-apprentice-ship training Select apprentices Ongoing training sessions at union for four years On-the-job training for four years	Higher satisfaction rates among union members Apprentices Achievement of journeyman status Active union member-ships Greater diversity of union membership	Proportion of enrolled apprentices who stay with the program Proportion of apprentices who complete the program, by demographic group Proportion of cohort that started program that eventually reach journey-man status Number of hours worked Proportion of union that is not non-Hispanic white and male

filled ver time. If employer requests are increasing, then you could assume that employers are increasingly turning to the union for their labor needs. The percentage of the requests that are filled is another way of considering employer satisfaction. Certainly, the union would want to keep track of the types of requests that were not filled at all or not to employers' satisfaction. Tracking these indicators over a period of time would reveal trends in the data. You may also want to standardize for economic conditions—employer requests could decrease in poor economic times, a condition beyond the union's control. To gauge the increase in employer satisfaction, you could hypothesize that at some point after the first cohort of trainees graduated from the program, those satisfaction indicators would increase. Obtaining a control group will be difficult, but consider using as a control union locals that do not have a training program.

You could take the same approach with indicators that reflect economic success of trainees and union members. You could track over time, perhaps monthly or quarterly, whether those who were trained increased their wages. You could also track whether those who went through the training program increased the number of hours that they worked. Perhaps as a comparison group, you could use union members with similar skills who did not go through the skills enhancement program, comparing their employability with that of program participants.

EXAMPLE 2:   **First Impressions Are Not What They Seem**

Operation Safety Net

Operation Safety Net is a program run out of a hospital in a small city. Reading its literature, one would logically conclude that the program's purpose is to provide the homeless population of its metropolitan area with free medical care. However, a closer look at the program shows that first impressions can be deceiving.

The PLM of Operation Safety Net (Table 2.3) reveals that the program actually has four goals: (1) to provide the unsheltered homeless population with access to health care services; (2) to train service leaders, focusing on medical workers, in how to treat the homeless; (3) to inspire service leaders, focusing on medical personnel, to serve the homeless; and (4) to create a new model for medical service, medical service delivery, and training for the benefit of the homeless population. The first goal is consistent with first impressions of the program. The other goals, though, are not the same as providing health care. Instead, they pertain to affecting how the health care system treats and provides care to the homeless population.

If the evaluators had stopped getting to know the program after the first impression and based an evaluation on such questions such as whether the homeless saw an increase in interactions with medical personnel, they would have missed the important aspect of the program's goals that pertain to how medical personnel are trained to deal with the homeless. In fact, the more interaction the evaluators had with the program, the more they came to believe that treating the homeless was somewhat incidental to the program. The program's real aim was to change the way the health care system dealt with the homeless. Training medical personnel to provide care to the homeless was a way to decrease barriers to service delivery, to increase empathy for the homeless, and to make the homeless an important constituency throughout the trainees' entire medical careers. The program's ultimate hope was that "graduates" would be inspired to replicate the program in the geographic areas where they would be practicing later in their careers.

The second and third goals of the program rest on the assumption that health care workers want to be involved in providing health care to the homeless. Implicit in that assumption is the assumption that the homeless have different health care needs and that health care workers will improve their skills in treating the homeless through the program activities.

Creating two independent program theories captures the two-fold aspect of this program. One theory relates to how the program improves the health status of the homeless (Figure 2.6). In evaluation terms, this part of the program is not very interesting. It should be of little surprise that if one increases the provision of medical services to a previously underserved population, the health status of the population will improve. This theory suggests that evaluators should limit themselves to considering whether the program actually found the unsheltered population and then whether the trainees were able to provide the

TABLE 2.3. Program Logic Model (Operation Safety Net).

Goals	Assumptions	Target Population	Inputs	Activities	Outputs	Outcomes
Provide the unsheltered homeless population with access to health care services	There is a significant unsheltered homeless population	Unsheltered homeless population in [CITY], focusing on the neighborhoods of [. . .]	Administrators, e.g., physicians, nurses, other clinicians (paramedics, podiatrists, dentists, psychiatrists, etc.), program managers, volunteers, outreach workers, case managers	For Goal 1 Locate unsheltered homeless population	Number of students who go through training	Improvements in the overall health conditions of the unsheltered homeless population
Train service leaders, with a specific focus on medical personnel, in providing services to the homeless	Many unsheltered homeless are without access to health care	The unsheltered homeless population in the towns of [. . .]	Funding from federal, state, and local governments, from private foundations, and from individual contributions	Perform health care assessment on unsheltered homeless patient	Number of unduplicated homeless who receive care through program	Increased number of medical personnel trained to provide health care to the homeless
Inspire service leaders to work with the homeless, with a specific focus on medical personnel	Better access to health care will make people healthier	Medical and nursing students and residents who are passionate about serving the poor	In-kind contributions of office equipment, medical supplies, pharmaceuticals, vans, office supplies, computer systems, and PDAs	Address the patient's immediate health care needs	Number of health care "visits" by program upon homeless	Increased number of medical personnel inspired to provide health care to the homeless
	Health care workers want to be involved in providing health care to the homeless	Medical and nursing students and residents who are required to participate in the program as part of their medical school training		Arrange for referrals and schedule appointments for patient to see other health care providers		Number of graduates of Operation Safety Net who
	There is a need for a model of serving the unsheltered homeless population			Provide preventative care to patient		
				Provide social work intervention		
				Refer to sources of free pharmaceuticals		
				Refer to cold weather shelters		

Create a new model for medical service delivery and training for the homeless	There is a need to inspire and train service leaders There is a need to develop a model for training health care workers in homeless issues and the specific challenges of providing services to the homeless Treating the homeless presents unique challenges	Other service providers with the capability of providing these services to areas and populations in need Other service leaders: non-medical school students, volunteers, outreach workers, health care administrators, civic leaders, community leaders	Access to the sponsoring hospital's resources, including support services, human resources, security, housekeeping, and insurance coverage of administrators Medical schools from which students are sent Cold weather facilities Reimbursement for services provided Material donation items (new white socks, underwear, boots, sleeping bags, and blankets) that are distributed to homeless	Provide assistance in signing up for free or subsidized insurance, if eligible For Goals 2 and 3 Recruit residents and students Train medical students through rotations and train nursing students through clerkships Provide all students with opportunities to observe training and treatment Provide residents with hands-on experience for medical, dental, and podiatric care	replicate the program where they practice medicine later in their careers

population with medical care. Evaluators would also consider the degree to which the eligible segment of this population was enrolled in free or subsidized health insurance. However, it would not be necessary to examine whether providing health care improves health, because a literature review would obviously show that this is a known linkage.

The other aspect of the program to be evaluated—the effect on those it trains—presents more of an evaluation challenge. Here, there is a jump in the theory between people being trained in providing health care to the homeless and being inspired to provide the homeless with care (Figure 2.7). The jump may be reasonable, but the connection will not happen with certainty or even near-certainty. The evaluation will likely concentrate on this theoretical linkage. To consider program integrity and the continued interest of the trainees, evaluators should track the number of people who enter and the number who complete the program. Evaluators could also check to see whether participants retain their knowledge of issues that impact the homeless.

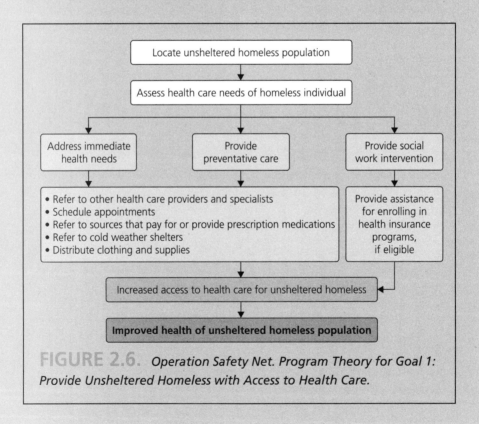

FIGURE 2.6. *Operation Safety Net. Program Theory for Goal 1: Provide Unsheltered Homeless with Access to Health Care.*

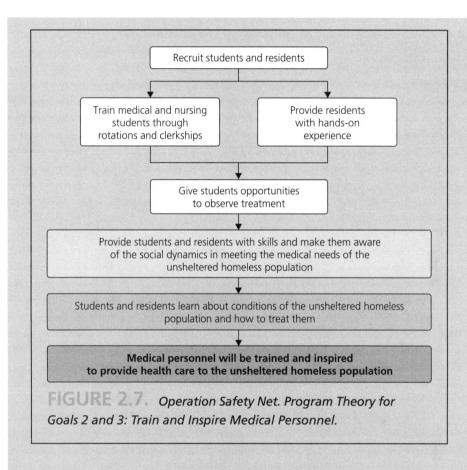

FIGURE 2.7. *Operation Safety Net. Program Theory for Goals 2 and 3: Train and Inspire Medical Personnel.*

EXAMPLE 3: Many Units of Analysis

Children's Health Insurance Outreach Program

A very different example of a program that operates at the community level comes from a child advocacy coalition. This program aimed to increase enrollment in the state's Child Health Insurance Program (CHIP), a program that offers health insurance for children in low-income families at little or no cost. The Child Advocacy Coalition (CAC) assumed, based on national studies, that many children in the community were eligible for but not participating in the health insurance program. The coalition assumed that the national data applied to the local situation, although it did not have any data at the local level to support this assumption.

To increase enrollment in the CHIP program, the advocacy coalition created "community collaboratives," small groups of nonprofit organizations that operate at the neighborhood level. Organizations that would belong to a "community collaborative" would include local churches, local offices of other need-based programs, food pantries, emergency feeding sites, schools, and so on. The coalition thought that if it shared information about CHIP with these small groups of nonprofit organizations that work at the neighborhood level, the nonprofit organizations would proceed to share that information with the people that they serve and the information would eventually reach parents and guardians of uninsured low-income children. The program also entailed the coalition working directly with families who requested assistance through the CHIP application process, answering questions, and helping them appeal any negative enrollment decisions.

Figure 2.8 displays the program theory for the coalition's Community Collaboratives approach. The coalition believed that if CHIP information was shared with the community collaboratives, then this would increase community awareness of CHIP, leading to increased individual or parental awareness of CHIP, thus increasing the perception and knowledge of the program's benefits. Also, increasing community awareness of the program (and how to enroll in the program) would decrease potential barriers to enrolling children in the program. Together, these improvements in awareness of and access to CHIP would increase the number of eligible children enrolled in the program. Having health insurance increases access to care, which in turn increases the use of health care services, which finally means that health needs are met and preventive care is used on a regular basis.

This program theory mixes the community level with the family level. The coalition essentially believed that creating higher community awareness "trickles down" to families. They also believed that the community collaboratives ultimately result in healthier children.

The literature that evaluators ought to review should pertain to the following questions:

- Does increased community awareness trickle down to needy families?
- Does decreasing barriers to program enrollment (not necessarily only health insurance programs, but also for other types of means-tested programs, such as Food Stamps, WIC, or housing assistance) ultimately result in an increase in program enrollment?

- Does increasing the perceived benefits of a program result in increased program enrollment?
- Does health insurance status affect utilization of health care services? Does it affect utilization of preventive care?
- To what degree does enrollment in governmental health insurance programs increase the proportion of people actually insured (or have the new enrollees simply gone from private insurance to public insurance)?

Literature that does not directly pertain to these questions should not be examined.

When deciding what to evaluate, if the literature on the second half of the program theory (links between health insurance and utilization of services and health) are very strong, then one does not need to form evaluation questions that will again prove what is already known. Instead, the evaluation should focus on what is theoretically unknown—the link between providing communities with information and families acting on the information that they may or may not have received through any community agency.

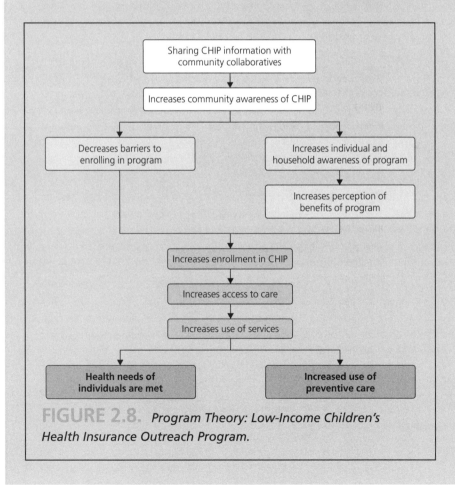

FIGURE 2.8.   *Program Theory: Low-Income Children's Health Insurance Outreach Program.*

EXAMPLE 4: A Program That Failed Because of a Faulty Assumption

The Housing Recovery Program

A city agency, through a public-private partnership, aimed to increase the rehabilitation of dilapidated homes by the city's low-income residents. The agency sponsored a program that was intended to offer residents loans that had, according to the agency, very favorable terms. Agency personnel were concerned about the program because participation fell well below the program's capacity and had decreased over time.

Many aspects of the terms of the loan seemed favorable, but there were many disincentives to participating in the program. Applicants had to go through a very time-consuming application process. If the loan pertained to the purchase of a house rather than the rehabilitation of a home that the applicant already owned, by the time the program processed the applicant's paperwork, the house could have been sold to another buyer.

The program insisted that any rehabilitation project comply with the Americans with Disabilities Act, even though nearly all homes in the low-income targeted areas were quite old. The unintended consequence of this specification was that it greatly increased construction costs—all doorways would have to be widened, bathrooms would have to meet ADA standards, and the house would have to be ADA accessible. The specifications seemed far-reaching, especially in a city with many houses built on hills where it was not uncommon to have to climb flights of stairs to get to a house.

Other possible reasons for the lack of applicants to the program included potentially unsuccessful marketing efforts. Further, the basis of the program was to improve the housing stock in low-income areas. It is difficult to convince people that taking on personal debt, even under favorable terms, in order to have the best house in a poor neighborhood is a wise financial move.

Delving into the details of the program using the PLM (Table 2.4) and examining some basic data on the terms of the loans and the number of applicants, the reason for the decline in applicants became readily apparent. The PLM shows that a major assumption of the program is that it will offer loans at favorable terms. Being government-run, the program was less able than private lenders to respond to a decrease in interest rates and a loosening in the availability of home equity lines of credit. At the time, interest rates had decreased and home equity lines of credit were readily available (which later led to the sub-prime mortgage crisis). The loan terms offered by the program, coupled with the specifications and regulations it imposed on applicants, made the program unattractive.

This program provides an excellent example of the fact that when programs truly fail, they usually do so because of incorrect or off-base assumptions that they have made about the environment in which they operate. Well-designed programs are based on realistic, accurate, well-thought-out assumptions about their environments. Programs that fail usually are designed poorly; even if implemented well, programs that make faulty assumptions usually cannot succeed.

In this case, the program seemed to be implemented well. The program administrators appeared to be doing everything right—they worked well with community groups, processed applications quickly, and took advantage of all opportunities for the program. However, outside of the administrators' control was the faulty basis for the program.

Evaluators provide a great service when they are involved in the design of programs. An experienced and good evaluator should be able to draw out the assumptions of a program and critically examine them. The program should try to provide as much evidence as possible so that the assumptions it makes are realistic.

TABLE 2.4. Program Logic Model (Housing Recovery Program).

Goals	Assumptions	Target Population	Inputs	Activities	Outputs	Outcomes
Stimulate the rehabilitation of deteriorated residential buildings	Individuals want to buy and live in homes in the city	All residential properties at least 20 years old within the city limits	Agency staff: • Director of housing (5% FTE)	Build public awareness of the program by sponsoring print ads on buses, mailing program brochures, and giving promotional presentations to neighborhood groups, realtors, and community organizations	Number of applicants Number of loans provided	Improvement in the housing stock of the city
Promote home ownership in targeted city neighborhoods	Individuals want to buy and rehabilitate houses older than 20 years and in need of repair	Individuals with houses in need of substantial repair who want to refinance to pay for the rehabilitation of the house	• Program manager (20% FTE) • Program officer (100% FTE)			Increased property values of HRP participating houses
Return vacant and underused properties to tax rolls	Private sellers are willing to wait for buyers to go through the HRP		• Program assistant (20% FTE)			Decrease in vacant and condemned houses
Eliminate vacant and underused housing	House rehabilitations will not occur without HRP		• Budget officer (10% FTE)	Screen applicants and when appropriate, provide combination mortgages and remodeling loans		Increase in the city's tax rolls
Diversify income mix of neighborhoods	Housing stock will remain vacant and underused without HRP		• Rehabilitation officers (45% FTE)			Increase in the income mix of neighborhoods
	HRP's interest rates are competitive		• Credit counselors (as needed)	Secure program funding from multiple sources,		
	Individuals are willing to accept HRP rehabilitation guidelines					
	Applicants exist who meet HRP requirements					

Borrowers are willing to go through the application process

A market exists for the agency's financial instruments, tax-exempt bonds

HRP funding from HUD and the State remains constant

Available housing stock meets HRP regulations

Public awareness of HRP exists

Contractors are approved and willing to rehabilitate the houses

Homeowners will reside in rehabilitated houses

Homeowners will repay agency when they sell or transfer title of their house

Funding:
- Federal ($1.15 million)
- State ($200K)
- Agency ($1.7 million)
- Banks
- Realtors (account for 20% of referrals to HRP)
- Agency office space
- City cable feature on HRP
- Lead inspectors
- Code inspectors
- Program Web site hosted by agency

e.g., Federal Community Development Block Grants, Federal Home Investment Partnerships Program, the state's Department of Community and Economic Development, and the municipal bond market

Determine where house is located and determine the structure of the loan

Assure that program's regulations are being applied appropriately to the rehabilitation project

EXAMPLE 5: Affecting Families and Communities

A Prenatal Care Program

A state sponsors a program aimed to improve the prenatal health of participants. Two interviews, one with program administrators who meet at bi-monthly program administrator network meetings, and another with two state-level administrators, resulted in the program theory.

Program activities start with staff assessing the needs and capabilities of clients, and then developing a care plan for the clients. The target population column of the PLM shows that the program aims to assist pregnant and postpartum women and their children under three. In order to participate in the program, the household income of the women cannot exceed 185 percent of the federal poverty threshold.

The program provides wraparound services to eligible pregnant women, aiming to improve their health and that of their babies not only through direct health interventions, but also by improving the family's financial security. The key to the program's success is that the program must accurately assess a mother's social and financial security and be able to directly respond to her needs. If the first assessment is inaccurate, then the program will fail its clients.

According to the program theory (Figure 2.9), if the program develops the client care plan, the women will receive appropriate services and referrals, increasing their access to health care. This will lead to increased awareness of health issues, which will further improve the chances that they will make health a higher priority for themselves and their families.

One arm of the program theory addresses the individual-family level, while the other arm addresses the societal level. At the individual-family level, if health is a higher priority, then there will be better birth outcomes, leading to an improvement in the long-term health of clients and their families. However, the long-term health improvement can also occur without better birth outcomes—it can occur directly from health becoming a higher priority. If there are long-term improvements in health, then there will be cost savings for the health care system.

At the societal level, if individuals make health a higher priority for themselves and their families, then the community's health awareness and public health knowledge will increase, improving the long-term health status of the community. This will ultimately also lead to cost savings for the health care system.

Colors are used to distinguish the arms of the program theory and to make it easier for audiences to digest the multiple theories of change being presented. In this example, the medium grey screen pertains to program activities and the white boxes reflect changes at the community level.

An evaluation plan for this program will likely cite literature to prove that the theoretical linkages between providing wraparound care and health care cost savings do exist. A good literature review should provide evidence for each of these linkages.

What remains to be shown is whether wraparound services were actually provided—that is, whether the causal chain of events was initiated. This program's evaluation plan would focus on the extent to which clients' needs were actually met. The issue of attribution, meaning how to attribute changes in clients' prioritization of their own and their families' health care, would be difficult to consider. In this real-world case, the program is offered to all low-income women in the state and had been for at least twenty years before the evaluation. There was no "control group." One might suspect that low-income pregnant women who do not participate in the program are fundamentally different from those who did. Those who participate may be needier or more interested in their well-being. If these women are more concerned about their health than those who did not participate in the program, then it is likely that even in the absence of the program these women would have better pregnancy outcomes simply because they were more willing to take care of themselves during pregnancy (for example, better nutrition, avoidance of high-risk behavior). This concern is reflected in the threat to internal validity of selection, discussed in the next chapter.

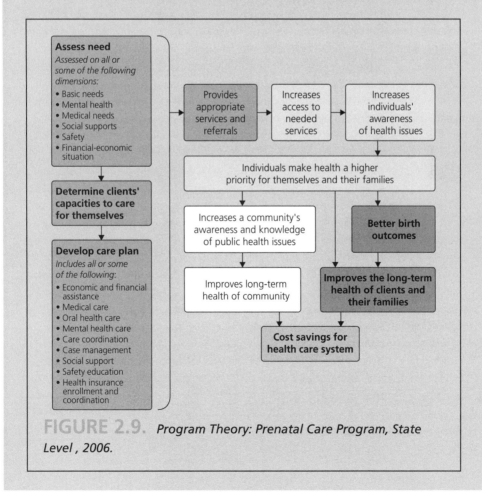

FIGURE 2.9. *Program Theory: Prenatal Care Program, State Level , 2006.*

EXAMPLE 6: Desperate Times Do *not* Call for Desperate Measures

The Magic Carpet Ride and the Traveling Party Program

Desperate to stop the outflux of the city's population, a foundation in the city sponsored a program that turned out to have a very weak design. This program is one of the weakest programs that I have ever seen, and I believe that the only reason that it was generously funded was because the city's leaders were desperate to stem the tide of out-migration from the city. To understand the desperation, one must understand the context of the program.

The city, in America's "rust belt," had suffered staggering losses in the 1970s when the industries upon which its economy was based, steel and manufacturing, suffered a large decline, leading to a decline in the city's population. By the 1990s, the city's population was less than half of what it was during its heyday—and between 1990 and 2000, U.S. Census data showed that the city's population had decreased by another 10 percent.

City and county leaders wanted to stop this trend, and were willing to try a variety of approaches. Although some efforts were worthy, others were not well thought out and were doomed to fail from the start. For example, one program, cynically referred to as the Magic Carpet Ride, took a handful of young professionals from the Silicon Valley area in California, flew them to the city for a weekend, and showed them the city's attractions in hopes that the visitors would relocate to the city. Predictably, that program, which was hyped by the local media, failed—because it was designed poorly and had unrealistic assumptions, chiefly, that a migration decision would be determined by a visit. The migration literature points to the importance of jobs and economic opportunities in the migration decision. The program did not address the economic opportunities that the young professionals would have in the city, as compared with their current opportunities in Silicon Valley or, for that matter, with other places in the United States.

At the local level, the Traveling Party Program evolved at about the same time as the Magic Carpet Ride. The Traveling Party Program in many ways was the theoretical cousin to the Magic Carpet Ride, but aimed toward the local rather than national level. The Traveling Party Program targeted very distressed neighborhoods in the city, rather than the entire city. The program aimed to revitalize these areas by sponsoring a large party in the neighborhood. Working on one neighborhood at a time, the program would find a building in the neighborhood, often abandoned but under rehabilitation, and use the building for the party. Often, electricity for the party came from a generator and there was no working plumbing in the building.

The program would sponsor a variety of artists to appear at the party—such as bands and other musicians, visual artists, or dancers. Alcohol would be served at the party. Hundreds of people would come to the party, a result of marketing efforts. The party was a one-night event and afterward the program would move on to another neighborhood. Two or three parties would be held annually.

Program designers hoped that throwing a party in a neighborhood would ultimately affect migration to the neighborhood. That is, by entering the neighborhood to attend the party, partygoers would be more likely to revisit the neighborhood and ultimately reside there, and their presence would revitalize the neighborhood. Two assumptions are implicit in this belief: first that the intensity of the intervention was sufficient—visiting a neighborhood at night for the purposes of attending a party will induce people to return to a distressed neighborhood and ultimately move there. The program also implicitly assumes that the partygoers are of a higher socioeconomic status than the neighborhood's current residents.

Having attended one of the parties, I became even more skeptical of the likelihood of the program's success. Because the parties were being held in economically distressed neighborhoods and so many people attended them (approximately one thousand attendees), and because alcohol was served, there was a substantial police presence both outside the party, to assure that people did not become crime victims, and inside the party, to assure that events were under control. To me, it seemed that being introduced to the neighborhood under these circumstances would not affect whether I returned to it under ordinary circumstances. The program failed, probably because of the assumption that its efforts were intense enough to affect where people chose to reside, and probably to a lesser degree because of the inauthenticity of the neighborhood experience during the party.

SUMMARY

Before evaluating a program, the evaluator needs to thoroughly understand it. Involving stakeholders to reach a description of the program is essential—if stakeholders don't recognize the program, they will not put the evaluation to use. Three models used to describe programs are presented in this chapter: program theory, the program logic model, and the program implementation model.

Program theory articulates the program's vision of how the program will cause change. It displays the causal chain of changes.

The program logic model (PLM) diagrams the operation of the programs in eight columns: Goals, Assumptions, Target Population, Inputs/Resources, Activities, Outputs, Outcomes, and Outcome Measures.

The program implementation model is similar to a flowchart. It sequences the program's activities to get a clear understanding of the program.

By using one of these models to describe a program, one can clearly see the opportunities for improvement and concise ways to evaluate the program's processes and outcomes.

KEY TERMS

activities   parsimony
assumptions   primary goals
goals   program implementation model
inputs   program logic model (PLM)
iterative process   program theory
operationalize   secondary goals
outcome measures   stakeholders
outcomes   target population
outputs   unit of analysis

DISCUSSION QUESTIONS

1. What are the common mistakes evaluators make when describing a program? How can you avoid making these mistakes?

2. Using one of the examples from the end of the chapter, create five interview questions to ask the stakeholders.

3. Describe how the models have further benefits to the program being evaluated.

CHAPTER

3

LAYING THE EVALUATION GROUNDWORK

LEARNING OBJECTIVES

After reading this chapter, you should be able to

- Describe summative and formative evaluations
- Understand the importance of choosing evaluation questions
- Be familiar with the advantages and challenges of the three types of evaluators

EVALUATION APPROACHES

There are essentially two approaches to evaluation: **summative evaluation** and **formative evaluation.** We often refer to summative evaluations as *the evaluation* and formative evaluations as *evaluatory activities.* Formative evaluation produces information that is fed back to decision makers who can then use the information to continuously improve the program. If a program is in an early stage, then certainly you would desire a formative evaluation. Compared to summative evaluations, formative evaluations sometimes place more of an emphasis on processes than outcomes, but the distinguishing feature between formative and summative evaluations is how the program or organization learns from the evaluation. Formative evaluation is used for making "data-driven decisions," which have the appearance of being impartial and dispassionate. However, this kind of evaluation is often used as a way to delay decision making until more can be learned about the issue.

A program need not be stable in order to utilize formative evaluation. In fact, formative evaluation is often used when there is flexibility in the program's design, when program personnel aim for continuous improvement, or when decision making about the program's design or implementation are on the horizon.

In contrast, summative evaluations are what I call "report card" evaluations, as they are usually done after the program has been completed. The information produced is not used to improve, but instead to determine the extent of the program's effectiveness. Summative evaluations often take the form of evaluation reports, where research is done on the intervention, a report is written, and the report is disseminated to relevant stakeholders (such as funders, program administrators, boards of directors, and so on). Pilot programs tend to use summative evaluations.

Summative evaluations tend to make program personnel very nervous. It is said that with respect to summative evaluation, there are two lies that are told at the start.

Evaluator to program director:

"Hello, I'm your evaluator and I'm here to help you improve your program."

Program director to evaluator:

"It's very nice to meet you."

This evaluation joke has some truth to it. Often, when people think of evaluation, they think of only the summative approach. I contend that if an evaluation is only summative and the program is ongoing, then both the evaluator and the program's stakeholders have missed the opportunity to improve the program.

Program staff feel nervous because a summative evaluation will be judging not only the program, but also their work—and to a great extent, they are correct. The ramification of this becomes that the staff then tries to present the program in the best light—for example, they spruce up the facilities, they may put in extra effort when the evaluator is present, and they may even discourage the clients who are not a good example of the strength of the program from coming in, and so on. If these strategies occur, the evaluator would get a biased view of the program and perhaps not ultimately be considering the program as it actually operated, but considering some special version of it.

Another problem with summative evaluation is how the results are used. If the program is found to be "successful," the results are flaunted. However, if the program is deemed unsuccessful, the results often get buried. It is the rare negative evaluation that becomes public. No funder likes it to be widely known that it wasted significant amounts of money and human capital on an unsuccessful program. There are exceptions, though. After the failure of the Heinz Endowments' "Early Childhood Initiative"—which cost the foundation over $20 million—the foundation, not satisfied with the initial evaluation of the program, hired Rand Corporation researchers to thoroughly investigate reasons for the initiative's failure. The Heinz Endowments made the monograph written on the initiative's failure, "A Noble Bet," publicly available (Gill, Dembosky, and Caulkins, 2002).

Although there are, in theory, clear distinctions between the summative and formative approaches to evaluation, in practice, the world is a bit different. What was intended to be a summative evaluation sometimes takes on the role of a formative evaluation. For example, an evaluation may be conducted on a program thought to be stable and inflexible, but once the report is read, stakeholders may see areas for improvement and decide to engage the program in ongoing evaluation activities. In this case, the summative evaluation acts as a formative evaluation.

Another somewhat superficial distinction is drawn between process-based and outcome-based evaluations. Process evaluations focus on the "how" of program delivery—and outcome evaluations emphasize the change in "clients" or "participants" that result from the program's activities. However, for some programs, especially for advocacy-type programs, the processes *are* the outcomes. Having contact with the targeted population (such as legislators or policymakers) may be the short-term goal of the program. It may be inappropriate, for example, to hold advocacy programs up to the standard of a changed vote on an issue.

FRAMING EVALUATION QUESTIONS

Now that the program has been described through its program theory and program logic model, the evaluator must plan the evaluation or evaluation activities. Before embarking on data collection and all of the potentially labor-intensive activities that evaluation can entail, it is vitally important to determine the appropriate evaluation questions. The evaluator must come to terms with funders or program personnel over the scope and depth of the evaluation and formulate concise evaluation questions.

Novice evaluators tend to ask a large quantity of evaluation questions about all aspects of the program, but the answers they get are frequently not informative. Sometimes, the most pertinent questions have not been asked or the answers to these questions are buried under the pile of material produced by the evaluation. Not asking the correct set of evaluation questions not only wastes monetary resources, but perhaps more importantly, can waste the goodwill, buy-in, and time of everyone involved in the evaluation. Before starting work on an evaluation, the questions must be narrowed down to the most parsimonious set.

Once the program description is finished, program personnel and the evaluator must come to consensus on the evaluation questions. During the informal interviews conducted in the process of program description, the evaluator should have asked stakeholders what questions they hope the evaluation will address, thus forming the universe of possible evaluation questions. This universe must be reduced until the evaluator and stakeholders agree on the scope and depth of the evaluation. This is not to say that there cannot be some flexibility as things proceed. Some questions that were not part of the initial universe of questions may emerge only once evaluators find answers to other questions. All parties involved should know and agree on the planned scope of the evaluation.

I have taught evaluation for approximately fifteen years. The course that I teach pairs up evaluation graduate students with local nonprofits. The students must create an appropriate practice evaluation plan for one of the nonprofit's programs by the end of the semester. At the beginning of the semester, when discussing the issue of how to decide upon evaluation questions, the students tend to think that this part of developing the evaluation plan will be simple. They quickly want to move on to the "real" part of the evaluation.

However, even three months into the semester, after informally interviewing clients and having described the program, the students often are still struggling with exactly what the evaluation questions should be.

It is rarely obvious what the evaluation questions should be. Whittling down the universe of possible questions to the smallest, most parsimonious set of questions can be a balancing act between satisfying the interests of various stakeholders and choosing a sound evaluation approach. In the best of all possible worlds, the evaluator would find answers to all pertinent questions about the program. Unfortunately, there are rarely enough resources to conduct such a comprehensive evaluation and deal with what would be an overload of information.

So, evaluators must trade off and prioritize the essential questions against those that are interesting but not absolutely necessary. Unless consensus is reached, any evaluation will likely fail because stakeholders will find it "off the mark" and irrelevant. If an evaluation is seen as irrelevant, then the results of the evaluation will not be used and time and resources would have been wasted.

The prioritization of questions may depend on the clout of the stakeholder who advocates for the question, the amount of time it would take to answer the question, the resources needed to answer the question, and how central the question is to the program's mission. Further, organizations usually have an idea of which processes and outcomes must be included in the evaluation rubric. After the universe of stakeholders is identified (see Chapter Two for a list of possible stakeholders), then representatives from all of these groups should be interviewed about their expectations for the evaluation; to conserve resources, this can be done during the initial informal interview.

People who order an evaluation are usually at the top of the program hierarchy—they could be program funders, executive directors, or the board of an organization. However, the audience for the evaluation usually includes all of the program's stakeholders, as well as potential participants of the program.

Each group of stakeholders will want the evaluation to have a different emphasis. Typically, funders want to know whether resources are being utilized wisely, and whether the program should be cut or expanded. Program directors want to know whether their efforts produce intended effects, and program personnel typically ask whether their efforts are appropriate—whether they could be more effective, and whether they are reaching the right people. Current clients want to know how the program is likely to affect them, and potential clients want to know how the program compares with other programs.

Informal interviews with stakeholders can clarify which evaluation questions are important, and which are not. How should you select representatives of the groups of stakeholders? Some people, such as the program funder, executive director, and program administrator, certainly should be contacted and interviewed. There exist other groups, such as program clients and alumni, that are too large to allow individual interviews. You must then carefully consider how to select interviewees from these groups. One method is to randomly choose individuals, and another approach is to choose individuals from the program's extremes—those who have benefited and those who seem not to have benefited; some who seemed pleased with the program, versus those who are not, and so on. Evaluators should elicit from stakeholders their expectations regarding the evaluation, with a goal of forming appropriate evaluation questions.

Typical evaluation questions include:

- How is the program being conducted?

- What is the program actually doing?

- How well does the program adhere to guidelines and the program plan as originally set?

- What kinds of outcomes does the program produce?

- Did the program cause the outcomes observed?

- Is the program worth the money it costs?

- How sustainable is the program?

- Should the program be continued, expanded, cut back, changed, or abandoned?

- Should people flock to it, sign up selectively, or stay away in droves?

- Does the program work for everybody or for only some kinds of people?

- Are the program results a fluke, or will similar programs produce similar results?

- Is the program replicable?

- Who are the program's constituents and advocates?

Answering these questions requires a rigorous evaluation approach. They cannot be answered using informal methods such as customer satisfaction surveys or anecdotes. Often, only the people who are very happy or very disappointed with a program respond to passive customer satisfaction surveys. Although they may reveal kinks in the process of service delivery, such surveys cannot reveal any long-term program impacts, and clients usually do not know how to gauge whether the program is successful. Further, staff cannot be relied upon to answer these typical evaluation questions because they are often optimistic about the impact of their efforts.

INSINCERE REASONS FOR EVALUATION

Sometimes, a program becomes engaged in evaluation for reasons other than program improvement. Evaluation can be used as a way to delay decision making, or as a way of collecting more information to support a decision that has been made de facto even before the evaluation has begun. In this way, the evaluation is used to give legitimacy to a decision.

Evaluation may also be used as a way of ducking responsibility for a decision. For example, administrators may know that there are not enough funds to support all of an organization's programs, but call for an evaluation to provide dispassionate evidence on which programs to cut.

An evaluation may be used as a way to glorify a program, or to provide a public relations opportunity. In this case, those ordering the evaluation may bear pressure on the evaluator to research only the potentially positive attributes of the program.

All of these circumstances have the potential to create an uncomfortable environment for an earnest evaluator. Therefore, from the beginning, the evaluator must develop a thorough understanding of the perspectives that stakeholders hold regarding the evaluation and the specific questions that they want to see answered.

WHO WILL DO THE EVALUATION?

When an organization is ready to embark on evaluation, it needs to decide who will lead evaluation efforts. An organization essentially has the choice of three different, but somewhat overlapping approaches to use:

1. An external evaluator who is new to the organization

2. An external evaluator with whom the organization has worked before

3. An internal evaluator on the organization's staff

These three choices can be viewed as being on a continuum, with pros and cons to each approach.

External Evaluators

External evaluators, hired on a contractual basis, have the appearance of impartiality, and because of this, consumers of this kind of evaluation may place greater credence in these results than in those of a report written by an in-house evaluator.

To find an outside evaluator, an organization may issue a Request for Proposals (RFP) and open up the evaluation activities for competitive bidding. The RFP usually indicates the scope of the evaluation, the time period, and the funding available for the evaluation. When posted on the American Evaluation Association's Web site, professional evaluators will become aware of the evaluation opportunity.

Sometimes the scope of the evaluation entails ongoing activities and the organization desires that the evaluator be "on call," or retained for some time period. Hiring this type of evaluator may prove difficult. The organization should search for someone local or nearby who has the flexibility and availability to work in this expert capacity. Before contracting with the evaluator, the organization should try to understand the evaluation approach to which the evaluator subscribes.

When hiring a new external evaluator, the organization or program can expect that the evaluator will need time to develop an understanding of the organization and program or initiative within it, the personalities involved, the culture of the organization, and the context of the program. The organization will need to help the evaluator develop this understanding, which can take some time, but this can be shortened if the evaluator chosen has experience working with similar programs and organizations.

The organization will need to open itself up to an "outsider," and therefore place trust in this outsider. For this reason, an organization is wise to request references from any potential evaluator, and the organization should inquire not only about the quality of past work, but also the quality of the relationship that an organization developed with the evaluator.

Because of the trust factor and the start-up costs incurred when contracting with a new evaluator, an organization often develops a relationship with an outside evaluator and becomes a repeat client. After the first contract, the outside evaluator will have gained valuable knowledge about the organization and *if all goes well,* the organization grows comfortable with the evaluator, who will then be the prime candidate for the organization's future Requests for Proposals. Some organizations may choose to bypass the RFP and not open the next evaluation up to competitive bidding—because they already have an evaluator with whom they are comfortable. In this way, such an external evaluator will have the "inside track" to a future RFP. In this case, there is a risk that the external evaluator will segue into a role close to that of the internal evaluator, although the external evaluator is never formally on the staff of the organization.

But note the caveat "if all goes well." Usually, if all goes well means that the evaluator constructively critiqued the program, pointed out areas where the program could improve, and performed analyses within her realm of expertise. However, a program may feel that "going well" means that the evaluator was relatively uncritical of the program. That is, the evaluator acted as a cheerleader rather than a critical examiner of the program.

Judging an evaluator's past performance may lead to a bias towards evaluators who are not as critical as they ought to be about a program. That is, the client may prefer, in the short-term, an evaluator who doesn't reveal blemishes in a particularly harsh light, even when they ought to be. Unless an evaluator has a steady source of clients, he may be reluctant to alienate a client, even if the program needs to be reworked considerably.

I witnessed an instance where a very influential foundation funded a multimillion dollar large-scale pilot project to make available high-quality child care in low-income communities. Embedded in the grant were funds for an outside evaluator. At midcourse presentations of the project, the evaluator glossed over the most basic of critical flaws in the program—that it simply did not attract participants, and many families who did enter the program did not stay with it for the expected amount of time. Evaluators who point out critical flaws early on provide the program with opportunities for improvement. Withholding such information can doom a program, and in this case, the program never did achieve a reasonable level of participation. Some believed that because the "outside evaluator" worked for a university that was also a recipient of the foundation's generosity, the evaluator was very reluctant to reveal that the program's theory and implementation were weak. The strong ties between the evaluator, university, and foundation may have jeopardized the presumed impartial role of the evaluator.

Internal Evaluators

Internal evaluators, who are usually on the staff of the program's organization, provide an alternative to external evaluators. Benefits of an internal evaluator include the evaluator's familiarity with the organization and sometimes even with a particular program, reducing the amount of time that it takes to get to know the program. The internal evaluator may also have access to organizational documents that an external evaluator may not have, giving her a better understanding of the organizational history and a particular program's context. An internal evaluator may have a better understanding of the personalities in the organization, and how, for example, the personalities affect the program's degree of success. For example, an administrator's personal charisma may influence the success of a program.

Conversely, it may be socially or politically difficult for an internal evaluator to be frank about problematic programs. For example, consider a program where an internal evaluator finds that a program is not being implemented as intended, possibly due to an administrator's negligence. This evaluator may find it difficult to highlight such problems. In the case of a weak program, an internal evaluator may put too much weight on outside forces, and in the case of a strong program, he may give too much credit to a program. An internal evaluator may be biased and should take precautions against such biases.

Because of the above social and political ramifications of evaluation activities, internal evaluators must be protected within the organization both for their sake and for the sake of the credibility of evaluation. They must be assured that their job security is unrelated to the results of an evaluation and that their compensation is only related to the *quality* of their evaluation activities, not the *results* of them.

The biggest strike against using an internal evaluator is the appearance of partiality. If one is interested in producing an evaluation report for an external funder or other external audience, the internal evaluator may be seen as being partial to the employer. If the appearance of impartiality is essential, then an external evaluator must be used. However, if evaluations will ultimately be used primarily for the internal purposes of program improvement, then an organization will have the flexibility to have evaluators on staff.

Small nonprofits usually do not have the funds to employ an in-house evaluator. Some organizations, especially those that run a wide assortment of programs and have multimillion dollar budgets and use evaluation primarily for internal purposes, would be wise to develop in-house evaluation capabilities, either by hiring employees with evaluation expertise, or by training current employees.

There are pros and cons of both external and internal evaluators. The most important thing about choosing an evaluator is deciding upon why the evaluation is needed. If an organization embarks on evaluation to please an external audience, then an external evaluator is most appropriate. However, if an organization embarks on evaluation for continuous improvement, if funds allow, and if the organization is large enough, then it may consider having an evaluator on staff or developing a long-term relationship with an external evaluator. When an evaluator is on staff, she needs to be given the freedom and job stability that would allow constructive criticism of particular programs.

If an organization chooses to use external evaluators, then it would be wise to somehow get evaluation expertise on its side. Sometimes, organizations issue RFPs that let the evaluators who submit proposals determine how the evaluation will be conducted. The risk in relying upon those who submit proposals to do the thinking for the organization is that the deliverable the organization receives may not ultimately be satisfactory with respect to the evaluation questions asked, methods used, and focus. Alternatively, an organization can design the evaluation plan itself, providing it has some evaluation expertise either on staff or retained, and then issue an RFP for evaluators to carry out the plan. An organization must decide whether it wants to be hands-on in the design of the evaluation, or whether it wants to leave that up to those who submit proposals. I advise organizations to work with an experienced evaluator in constructing evaluation plans, and then issue an RFP for the evaluation plan to be carried out.

CONFIDENTIALITY AND OWNERSHIP OF EVALUATION ETHICS

Before embarking on evaluation, an organization or client and evaluator ought to consider the confidentiality of the evaluation and intellectual property rights. It is best if these issues are settled and made explicit at the outset.

Regarding ownership of reports and data collected for analyses, normally, *the entity that pays the bill "owns" the evaluation and the data.* If a funder provides an organization with a grant that includes funds for an evaluation, the organization normally owns the report and any data that result from the evaluation. In this case, the organization will provide the funder with a copy of the evaluation report; the evaluator is obligated to the organization, not to the funder.

In contrast, a funder may hire (or have on staff) an evaluator who conducts an evaluation of a program that the funder directly sponsors. In this case, the funder owns the data and the report, and chooses whether to share the information with the organization.

I can think of no case where the evaluator owns the report or the data. Unfortunately, I am aware of cases where evaluators believe that they own the data or reports. Such situations can quickly get ugly and have legal consequences.

Not owning reports and having to keep them confidential can put an evaluator in a somewhat professionally precarious position. The evaluator's allegiance should be to the organization or to the funder, depending on the circumstances. This means that the evaluator cannot take it upon herself to distribute an evaluation report. The only exception to this is when, in the course of the evaluation, egregious wrongdoing is discovered. Then, the evaluator may come under whistle-blower protection and release a report or findings on his own. The evaluator should understand, though, that releasing a report can be professionally risky. I would not advise doing so unless one clearly came under whistle-blower protection and had sought legal advice prior to the release.

All data collected in an evaluation should be kept confidential, unless the evaluator has an explicit agreement with a subject for the data not to be confidential, informed consent should also be considered. (Chapter Seven, "Collecting Data," provides more information on this topic.)

BUILDING A KNOWLEDGE BASE FROM EVALUATIONS

A recent trend in evaluation is to try to use the results to develop a better understanding of the efficacy of interventions. This perspective adheres to the principle that understanding which programs work and which do not will ultimately allow for more effective programs to be designed.

Although this perspective may seem reasonable and theoretically appropriate at first, it has a critical flaw—the unavailability of negative evaluations. Most negative evaluations—those that show that a program did not produce its intended effects—are not shared, or are not widely shared. Often, program stakeholders do not want to share a negative evaluation. Funders are not eager to advertise that they wasted money, the people who implemented the program do not want to publicize poor findings, and nearly everybody who would ultimately be responsible for dispersing the evaluation report would prefer that it be buried.

The paucity of information available on negative evaluations makes it impossible for a true knowledge base to develop. If one judges the efficacy of a type of intervention only on the basis of positive evaluations, then one has a biased view of what works and what doesn't, and one may erroneously conclude that an intervention always works, when in fact, it often does not. One may overestimate the desired effects of initiatives.

The *publication bias* is that positive evaluations are more likely to be published than those that have conflicting results, or reports that show that programs have no effect or are poorly implemented. This bias skews our understanding of interventions, and for this reason, it is important to try to include both positive and negative evaluations when developing an understanding of the efficacy of types of interventions.

HIGH STAKES TESTING

Increasingly, outcome-based evaluation is being used as the basis for making important decisions—such as distributing funds, ranking organizations, rewarding staff, and even rewarding schools. High stakes evaluations occur when evaluation is relied upon to make important decisions about a program's survival.

Usually, high stakes evaluation entails some form of high stakes testing, which occurs when results are used to make decisions with large ramifications. The following is the American Evaluation Association's position on high stakes testing on pre-K–12 students:

> High stakes testing leads to under-serving or mis-serving all students, especially the most needy and vulnerable, thereby violating the principle of "do no harm." The American Evaluation Association opposes the use of tests as the sole or primary criterion for making decisions with serious negative consequences for students, educators, and schools. The AEA supports systems of assessment and accountability that help education.

> —American Evaluation Association [2002]

The essential worry regarding high stakes testing is that putting too much emphasis on a test can lead to a weak evaluation and distort behavior around the test. A weak evaluation can result because the evaluation becomes entirely outcome-based, and unless those outcome measures perfectly reflect the goals of the program, the reliance on high stakes testing will not improve the program. For example, if the outcome is intended to be improvements in a student's mathematical ability, then the test needs to perfectly measure the theoretical construct of "mathematical ability."

If people believe that critical decisions will be based on the results of a test, then behavior around the test may be distorted. For example, teachers may start "teaching to the test"—that is, teaching students only material that will be on the test and teaching students how to take tests—rather than teaching a comprehensive curriculum, which may include topics not specifically on the test. Other examples of distorted behavior include encouraging people who may not do well on the test to be absent on the testing day, and encouraging test-takers to somehow behave differently for the test (such as to eat sugared cereal for breakfast if the test is given in the morning, which has been suggested to improve test performance). Also, taking prep courses for tests distorts the effectiveness of the test in measuring the desired construct (for example, mathematical ability) rather than the construct of one's familiarity with the test itself.

THE EVALUATION REPORT

Evaluation reports usually have similar outlines. Carole Weiss has suggested one outline, which is reproduced here (Weiss, 1998).

I. Summary of Study Results
   A. Questions addressed
   B. Brief description of program
   C. Main findings
      1. Concise summary of findings
      2. Implications
      3. Recommendations for the particular audiences (program improvement, policy action, etc.)

II. Problem with Which the Program Deals
   A. Size, scope, seriousness, trends over time
   B. Prior efforts to deal with it

III. Nature of the Program
   A. Goals and objectives
   B. Activities
      1. Original plan of activities
      2. Actual program activities
         a. Content
         b. Frequency
         c. Intensity
         d. Changes over time
         e. Consistency with, changes from, original program design
   C. Context
      1. Sponsorship of the program
      2. Setting(s)
         a. Community
         b. Site
         c. Facilities

      3. History of the program

      4. Funding

   D. Beneficiaries

      1. Number and characteristics

      2. How recruited

      3. Length of stay in program

      4. Dropouts

      5. Other relevant data

   E. Staff

      1. Number and characteristics

      2. Length of time with program

      3. Other relevant characteristics

IV. Nature of the Evaluation

   A. Central questions

   B. Conduct of the study

      1. Study design

      2. Time period covered

      3. Methods of data collection (brief; detail in appendix)

      4. Methods of analysis (briefer; detail in appendix)

   C. Results

      1. Findings

      2. Limitations to the findings

      3. Conclusions

      4. Interpretation

   D. Recommendations for action

V. Comparison with Evaluations of Similar Programs (optional)

VI. Suggestions for Further Evaluation (optional)

VII. Acknowledgments

VIII. Appendices

    A. Methodology

    B. Tables of data

    C. Transcripts of selected narrative material

Any report will include an executive summary, and many will read only this; thus it is vital that the executive summary be well-written and concise.

Section II, the *Problem with Which the Program Deals,* and much of Section III, the *Nature of the Program,* will come directly from the informal interviews. The program description—the program theory and program logic model—will take up most of Section III. One could present the program theory and program logic model at the beginning of Section III, and a commentary along with them that walks the reader through the theory and logic of the program. Within this section, the evaluator would note any of the program's potential vulnerabilities and strengths.

The examination of data begins in Section III-D, where it is recommended that the evaluator consider the characteristics of the clients or beneficiaries of the program. Section III-E considers characteristics of the program's staff and personnel.

It isn't until Section IV that the *Nature of the Evaluation* is discussed. This section would discuss how the evaluation questions were formed. Section IV-C presents results of the examination of data.

In this outline, it becomes apparent that for the evaluation to have weight, it needs to be put in the context of the program. Further, describing the program is of utmost importance, as is putting the program in its environmental and historical context.

Once the program has been described, the context of the program part of the report has been drafted, and all agree on the evaluation questions, we can move on to how to show that the program has caused change. Chapter Four addresses what it means to prove or show causation.

SUMMARY

There are two approaches to evaluation: summative and formative. Summative evaluations are usually done after the program has been completed and are used to determine the program's effectiveness. Formative evaluations produce information that decision makers use to improve the program.

It is vitally important to determine appropriate evaluation questions. The evaluator and stakeholders must agree on the scope and depth of the evaluation by agreeing on the questions. Without agreement, the evaluation will fail because stakeholders will find it irrelevant.

There are three types of evaluators an organization can choose to perform an evaluation: an external evaluator new to the organization, an external evaluator with prior experience with the organization, or an internal evaluator. The most important step about choosing an evaluator is determining why the evaluation is needed.

KEY TERMS

evaluation reports

external evaluators

formative evaluation

high stakes evaluations

high stakes testing

internal evaluators

outcome evaluation

parsimony

process evaluation

publication bias

summative evaluation

DISCUSSION QUESTIONS

1. Describe the difference between summative and formative evaluations.

2. What are the drawbacks of having too many evaluation questions? How can you drill down to the most important questions?

3. What are the pros and cons of using an external evaluator? An internal evaluator?

4. If you were using an external evaluator, how much detail would you put into the Request for Proposals?

CHAPTER

CAUSATION

LEARNING OBJECTIVES

After reading this chapter, you should be able to

- Define necessary and sufficient causation

- Describe how definitions of variables can greatly impact conclusions

- Understand the importance of intervening variables

- Describe how anticipating the effects of a program will affect data collection

- Articulate the advantages and disadvantages of continuous versus categorical variables

Program evaluation differs from statistics in one critical way—causation. Evaluation, especially summative, outcome-based evaluation, is done to examine whether a program or policy *causes* a change. If the intervention being examined does not cause a change, then there exists no justification for the intervention.

In contrast, statisticians examine data to investigate whether the null hypothesis of no association between change and intervention can be rejected. When this hypothesis can be rejected, it may seem likely that the intervention is associated with change, but statisticians cannot fully determine whether the intervention caused the change beyond all doubt. Statistical analysis skirts the edges of causation, but summative program evaluation is often done specifically to investigate whether a causal relationship exists between an intervention and outcome.

Those who design programs or interventions do so because they believe that, ultimately, the intervention will produce, or *cause* a change. But what does it mean to cause a change?

Cause can be interpreted in many ways. In this chapter, we consider the meaning of causation and its various theoretical forms. The chapter's goal is to peel away at various forms of causation. We start with two aspects of causation: necessary and sufficient.

NECESSARY AND SUFFICIENT

Evaluators can consider an intervention necessary and sufficient in the following ways:

- Is the program **necessary** for the change in the outcome to occur? That is, could the change have occurred without the program?

- Is going through the program **sufficient** for seeing a change occur? Do all people who go through the program change?

Consider the change or outcome that stakeholders desire a program to produce. In the case of a substance abuse program, the intended outcome could be a change in the likelihood to abuse drugs or alcohol; in the case of an opera appreciation program the intended outcome could be a positive change in one's regard of opera; in the case of a "dress for success" program, the intended outcome could be an improvement in one's employment prospects; or in a math tutoring program, a change in one's understanding of mathematical concepts. Each of these programs desires to produce a desired outcome, or seeks to cause a change.

We would say that the program is *necessary* for the change if the desired outcome could *only* occur if the intervention caused it to occur; thus the change would be seen *only* in cases that had gone through the program. This is the definition of a causally necessary program.

Very few programs live up to this stringent view of causation. Clearly, people can develop an appreciation for opera without going through an opera appreciation program, students can understand mathematics without a math tutoring program, and employers can be satisfied with a labor union without an apprentice program. Often, there are many ways for the desired outcome to have been achieved, the program being just one of the ways. People may have been instilled with characteristics that allow them to possess the desired outcome even in the absence of the intervention. Or, they may have gone through another program, or have acquired information in a variety of ways, none of which have anything to do with the program being evaluated. Labor market conditions may have changed so that everybody becomes more employable, not only those who completed an employment or "dress for success" program. So, making the case that a program is necessary becomes difficult, and a sound quasi-experimental design is needed to make the causal connection.

With respect to the concept of sufficient, one would say that a program is *sufficient* to produce the desired outcome in situations where one is guaranteed to have the outcome if one went through the program. There may be cases where the outcome is not observed, even among those who went through the program. In these cases, the program is insufficient. There may be other cases where the outcome was produced even in the absence of the program. If a program is sufficient to produce an outcome, then going through a program will assure that the outcome occurs, even though the outcome can occur in the absence of the program.

If a program is **necessary and sufficient**, then the outcome can *only* be produced by the program or intervention, and, if one went through the program, the outcome would *always* be produced. Given this definition, it is clear why few, if any, interventions live up to this level of causation. I can think of no program where (a) the outcome could *only* be produced by the program, (b) there does not exist a single case when the outcome exists without having gone through the program, and (c) the program will certainly produce the outcome in all of its participants.

A two-by-two matrix illustrates the concepts of necessary and sufficient. In the cells of the matrix are the number of observations that display the outcome.

In the case where the program is ***necessary,*** then one will never observe the outcome among nonparticipants of the program (Table 4.1). Therefore, all nonparticipants, whatever the number, will fall into the *no program/no outcome cell.* Among program participants, the program will be enough to produce the outcome for some, but not for others. Therefore, some participants will fall into the *yes program/no outcome* cell, while others will fall into the *yes program/yes outcome* cell. That the *no*

TABLE 4.1. **A Program That Is Necessary but Not Sufficient.**

Did one go through the program?	Is the outcome observed?	
	No	**Yes**
No	All nonparticipants	0
Yes	Some participants	Some participants

program/yes outcome cell has zero observations is a telltale sign that the program may be necessary to produce the outcome.

If a program is **sufficient** to produce the outcome, then all program participants will display the outcome (Table 4.2). Hence, all participants belong in the *yes program/ yes outcome* cell and the number zero belongs in the *yes program/no outcome* cell. There will never be a case where a participant does not possess the outcome. Among nonparticipants, the outcome may or may not be exhibited, because the relationship only considers sufficiency, not necessity. Therefore, some cases of nonparticipants will fall into the *no/no* cell, while others will fall into the *no/yes* cell.

In the **necessary and sufficient** program, one will observe zeros in the *no program/ yes outcome* cell and the *yes program/no outcome* cell (Table 4.3). That is, considering the participation status rows separately, nonparticipants will never exhibit the outcome because the program is necessary, and participants will always display the outcome because the program is sufficient. Zeros in the other two cells complete the matrix.

TABLE 4.2. **A Program That Is Sufficient but Not Necessary.**

	Is the outcome observed?	
Did one go through the program?	No	Yes
No	Some nonparticipants	Some nonparticipants
Yes	0	All participants

TABLE 4.3. **A Program That Has a "Necessary and Sufficient" Relationship with the Outcome.**

	Is the outcome observed?	
Did one go through the program?	No	Yes
No	All nonparticipants	0
Yes	0	All participants

The above examples are a gross but useful simplification of how evaluators typically consider data. Complications arise, even in this grossly simplified display of data. In order to put data into this neat two-by-two matrix, you must first have a definition of program participants and an observed outcome. That is, participants and outcomes are dichotomous variables—they have two (dichotomous) categories—yes or no. The real world, though, is not generally dichotomous. Often, we are dealing in a world where the data are nuanced, variables are continuous rather than discrete, and we need to make decisions about definitions.

The definitions of variables can ultimately impact the causal conclusions drawn. For example, defining who is and is not a program participant seems trivial at a first glance—those who went through the program are participants, and those who did not are nonparticipants. However, there is a grey area. How to classify someone who started the program but didn't finish it? Is a program participant defined as someone who completed every aspect of the program? At what level of participation is a client defined as a participant?

Likewise, defining whether an outcome is present or absent is also tricky. At what level of the outcome measure has the desired outcome occurred?

To illustrate the importance of the decisions surrounding the classification of data, in the chart below, we have constructed fictional data on the number of minutes parents

Time (minutes) spent reading with child	Test score
0	280
0	300
0	320
0	340
5	350
5	370
5	375
5	380
10	400
10	415
10	420
10	440
15	450
15	450
15	460
15	480
20	500
20	550
20	600

spend reading with a child and the child's test scores. A program aims to increase children's reading ability by encouraging parents to read with their children. In this example, we explore the causal relationship between the intervention (parental time) and the outcome (a child's test scores). We see that children whose parents do not read to them have scores ranging from 280 to 340 and those with parents who spend twenty minutes have scores ranging from 500 to 600. On the surface, there seems to be a correlation.

Next, we split the intervention and the outcome into categories. At first, we define a "low" amount of reading time as anything less than ten minutes, and a "high" amount of time as ten minutes or more. Likewise, we define a "low" test score as anything less than 400 and a "high" test score as 400 and above.

When we classify cases according to these definitions, we get the "matrix shown in Table 4.4.

The figures in the cells of this matrix suggest that whenever there is a low amount of time spent with a child, the test score is low, and whenever there is a high amount of time spent with the child, the test score is high. There are no cases where a child who spends a low amount of time with a parent receives a high score, and where a child who spends a high amount of time receives a low score. This fact suggests that reading with a child may have a *necessary and sufficient* relationship with test scores. That is, in order for a child to have a high test score, the parent must read to the child, and if the parent does not, the child is doomed to low test scores.

The interpretation of categorical data can change simply by changing the definitions of the categories used. To demonstrate this point, in the next case, we use the same data but define a low amount of time as ten minutes or less, and keep the same definition of a low test score—any score less than 400. When we modify only the definition of the amount of time spent, the matrix in Table 4.5 results.

The results of this categorization make it appear as if reading with a child for a longer amount of time is sufficient to produce high test scores—but isn't necessary. There are cases where a parent spent a low amount of time with the child and the child scored highly on the test.

TABLE 4.4. **Cutoffs Suggest a Necessary and Sufficient Relationship.**

Time spent reading with child	Test Score	
	Low (<400)	High (400+)
Low (<10 minutes)	7	0
High (10+ minutes)	0	11

TABLE 4.5. **Cutoffs Suggest a Sufficient but Not Necessary Relationship.**

Time spent reading with child	Test Score	
	Low (<400)	High (400+)
Low (10 minutes or less)	7	4
High (>10 minutes)	0	7

In this third case, we modify the definition of a high test score to be at least 500, and the definition of a high amount of time remains at more than ten minutes. When we do this, then the matrix in Table 4.6 results, and it appears that reading with a child is necessary but not sufficient for high test scores.

These three simple examples demonstrate that changing the cut points of variables in an analysis can change the interpretation of the data. When one performs a linear regression using the data, one sees that the variable "time spent reading with a child" explains 90 percent of the variation in test scores and that for every additional minute spent reading, the test score increases by nearly 11 points, a relationship which shows statistical significance. However, when we think of the possible causal relationship between reading time and test scores, we draw different conclusions, depending on how we divide the continuous data into categories.

In order to avoid arbitrary conclusions, you need to carefully consider the cut points of categories. When converting continuous data into categorical data, you should be able to substantively and theoretically justify the boundaries of the categories. If the boundaries are determined arbitrarily and there is no substantive justification for the categories, then what the data reveal and the conclusions you make will also be

TABLE 4.6. **Cutoffs Suggest a Necessary but Not Sufficient Relationship.**

Time spent reading with child	Test Score	
	Low (<500)	High (500+)
Low (10 minutes or less)	11	0
High (> 10 minutes)	3	4

arbitrarily formed. Decisions made about the definitions of categories have ramifications throughout the remainder of the analysis and the conclusions drawn from the data analysis. In the above simplified case, we see how we could come to different conclusions about the nature of the causal relationship between variables and outcomes.

It may seem that the solution, then, is to keep data in its continuous form. Statistically that might make sense, but in program evaluation we usually want to comment on the effectiveness of a program on participants versus comparable non-participants. Participation is usually defined as dichotomous—either one does or does not participate. Participation in a program will almost always be considered as categorical and not continuous.

On the outcome side the question in summative evaluation is often whether the participants show success as opposed to not showing any success or being partially successful.

Many funders' grant applications require that programs set "targets," which are sometimes called "benchmarks." The program then is held to these targets, and success is defined as whether the program meets the targets. There are many problems with this approach. First, applicants, thinking that setting grandiose targets in the application will result in a higher probability of funding, set the targets too high. The naïve funder may reward this type of "pie in the sky" target setting—but if the program's success is measured against this high threshold, it may ultimately be deemed unsuccessful.

Conversely, a few applicants will set their thresholds too low, knowing that the program's success will ultimately be judged against these thresholds. This is likely to be the case only among programs that feel secure in their chances of receiving funding—such as repeat grantees or grantees who may have a monopoly on satisfying a foundation's funding priority.

Sometimes, measures of success are set by people who have little expertise in the field. For example, I once saw businessmen define success for a preschool program. This essentially results in arbitrary targets.

My preference is that programs aim for continuous improvement in their processes, with the expectation that if the program's theory is sound and logic tight, improved processes will result in better outcomes. In the best of all worlds, targets would not be set a priori. However, knowing that many funders want targets to be set before a grant is handed over, my preference would be for targets to be based on the program's past experiences. In the case of new programs, it might be impossible to set realistic targets.

The causal connection between two variables can depend on the definitions used to create categories, and more often than not, evaluating programs becomes an exercise in examining the relationship between categorical variables. Evaluators should be able to justify the definitions of the categories created.

Another aspect of causation concerns how the presence or absence of other factors influences the relationship observed between the cause and effect of interest. The observed relationship between X (cause) and Y (effect) may be influenced by whether other factors are present. Some other factors may dampen or amplify the magnitude of the observed relationship between cause and effect.

Let us consider cases where the cause is denoted as X, the effect as Y, and an intervening variable as I. The three variables form a triangle. Different relationships between X and I, X and Y, and I and Y will result in various erroneous conclusions about the true relationship between X and Y. Consider the following three cases.

Case 1. Overestimating a Program's Effectiveness Because of the Presence of an Intervening Variable. In this case, X actually is positively related to Y—when X increases Y also increases, and conversely, when X decreases Y also decreases (Figure 4.1). However, X also has a positive relationship with I, an intervening variable that has an independent, positive relationship with Y. Thus, when X increases, I increases, and an increase on I results in an increase on Y, independent of X's increase on Y. If you do not take into account the independent impact of I, then you will erroneously overstate the magnitude of the effect that X has on Y. In the simplest case, the ultimate effect on Y will be additive—it will be the sum of X's effect on Y and X's effect on I, which then influences Y. However, you cannot assume that the two independent effects are simply additive—they could be multiplicative, or have some other functional form.

Case 2. Underestimating a Program's Effectiveness Because of the Presence of an Intervening Variable. As in the first case, X is positively correlated with Y (Figure 4.2). However, X is negatively correlated with I—when X increases, I decreases, and I positively affects Y. The net result here, if you only examine X and Y without considering the dampening effect of I, is that you would underestimate the impact of X on Y. In the most extreme case, it would seem that there is no relationship between X and Y, when, in fact, there is. This case is also known as drawing a false negative conclusion. In the extreme, you could erroneously conclude that X does not impact Y because the effect of I on Y negates the impact of X on Y.

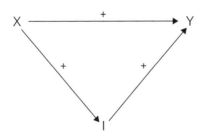

FIGURE 4.1. *Overestimating a Program's Effectiveness Because of the Presence of an Intervening Variable.*

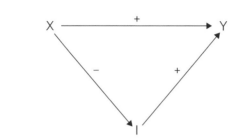

FIGURE 4.2. *Underestimating a Program's Effectiveness Because of the Presence of an Intervening Variable.*

Case 3. Misestimating a Relationship Between X and Y. One may erroneously interpret a situation as X causes Y, when in fact what happens is that X causes I, which in turn causes Y (Figure 4.3). In this case, there may seem to be a correlation between X and Y only when I is present. But when I is absent, there is no relationship between X and Y. If one observes X and Y only in the presence of I, then it would be easy to misinterpret the relationship between X and Y. If the program has only operated in circumstances where I is present, then it will seem that the program is effective. However, if the program is implemented in an environment where I is not present, then it is likely that the program will fail.

Intervening variables are important to consider because their presence or absence can cloud the true relationship a program has with its outcomes. If the program purely causes a change to occur, then it must do so in the absence of intervening variables.

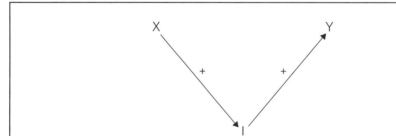

FIGURE 4.3. *Misestimating a Relationship Between X and Y.*

TYPES OF EFFECTS

Another aspect of causation pertains to the type of effect or outcome one anticipates the program will cause. We can think of this in terms of how long it takes for the outcome to appear, the sustenance of the intervention's effect on the outcome, and the functional form of the effect. All three aspects of the effect should be considered prior to collecting data on effects. The type of effect that you anticipate will relate to the length of time that data are collected, and the length of intervals between data collection. There exist a number of scenarios about which evaluators need to be cautious.

Lagged Effects

Some effects may appear immediately, while others may take some time to appear, or be lagged. Before starting with data collection, you should consider how much time it would take for the effect to appear. If an effect will take time to appear and you collect data too soon, then even if the program ultimately impacts participants, the data will suggest that it has no impact. The effect will appear after the data have been collected, and the evaluation of the intervention will suggest that it has been ineffective.

Lagged effects are difficult to attribute to the intervention. There may have been events that also could have produced the effect that occurred between the intervention and the effect.

Permanency of Effects

Similarly, some effects are long-lasting, while others may be short-lived. If an effect is short-lived, then one must collect evidence before the effect wears off. Evaluators refer to impacts that wear off as **discontinuous** (for example, people who go though a smoking cessation program and reduce smoking for a length of time, but then return to smoking). Conversely, effects that last forever are referred to as **continuous effects.** Usually, programs that provide skills training have continuous effects, although the skills may atrophy to some degree if not used after the program.

Functional Form of Impact

Some effects may exhibit themselves as a change in slope of an existing trend, a change in intercept of the trend, or a change in the functional form of the trend (Figure 4.4). For example, a tutoring program may modify the pace at which children learn, which would be exhibited by an increase in the slope of the functional form. Or, perhaps the program exists to aid a class with a particularly difficult issue. The children may exhibit a change in the intercept, or a one-time increase in their knowledge, but their overall learning pace may not be affected. Finally, an effect may be manifested in the change of a functional form of the effect. For example, rather than learning happening in a linear way, where children's test scores (if this is the chosen outcome indicator) increase at a rate of 5 percent per semester, we see that the increase in scores occurs logistically, or perhaps alters a seasonal pattern that had existed.

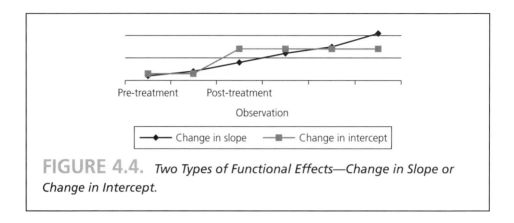

FIGURE 4.4. *Two Types of Functional Effects—Change in Slope or Change in Intercept.*

How one anticipates that the effects of the program will manifest will have an impact on the type of data collected, the length of time that data collection goes on, and intervals at which data will be collected. Therefore, it is critically important that the evaluator consider the impact anticipated from the intervention.

Another way in which the anticipated effect influences data collection is in **categorical** versus **continuous data.** If data on effects are collected in terms of categories, there is a chance that even if an intervention had an effect, the effect may not be observable because participants did not change their behavior enough to warrant moving into the next category.

For example, an evaluator may decide to collect income information categorically, and may be interested in determining if households that participate in an anti-poverty intervention move out of poverty. In this case, income data may be collected to reflect whether the household is below poverty, between 100–185 percent of poverty, and so on.

A participating household may have seen its income increase, but not to the extent that the household moves from one category to the next. If the data are collected categorically, then the program may seem to have no effect. However, if the data were collected continuously (where households were asked the dollar amount of income rather than their income category), then in the analysis, you could examine increases in income, rather than whether a participant moved from one category to the next. That is, collecting data in categories often constricts the analysis at a later date and can mask real changes that participants may have made. Collecting data in their rawest, noncategorical form allows for more flexibility in the analysis, which may uncover some unanticipated effects.

A non-fictional example of this phenomenon is considering the effectiveness of the federal food stamp program. One way to consider its effectiveness is to determine the extent to which the program increases spending on food among participating households. When researchers look at the program in this way, they find that for every dollar in assistance the program provides, food spending increases by about ten cents. Looking at the program this way is to consider the program in a continuous way.

Another way to study the program is to examine the extent to which it increases food spending to a level that a household could achieve a nutritionally sufficient diet. The U.S. Department of Agriculture (1999) defines this level as the Thrifty Food Plan, attaching a dollar amount to the cost of the Thrifty Food Plan. Instead of measuring the effect of food stamps by looking at the degree to which food expenditures increase, you can examine whether households using food stamps have a higher likelihood of achieving the Thrifty Food Plan. Research examining food stamps in this way has found that the program has little impact on households that receive only a small amount of subsidy from the food stamp program.

Another aspect of causation to consider is **spectacular causes** and **spectacular effects.** It is possible that small degrees of the causal variable, or small doses of the program or intervention, can produce very large effects. Conversely, it is also possible that large doses of the cause can produce small effects. Sometimes, planners think that intense interventions will produce large effects. This is not necessarily the case. There may be a "tipping point," below which the intervention will seem to have no effect, a threshold at which the intervention will seem to have a great effect, and above which the intervention may seem to have no additional effect. You should be cognizant of the possibility of a tipping point situation, and create data collection approaches that will be sensitive and be able to detect the existence of such a situation.

When planning a program and considering evaluation, be aware of the various types of causal relationships that might exist. Before collecting data on possible programmatic outcomes, consider all of the issues discussed above.

SUMMARY

Classifying data greatly impacts conclusions. Changing the boundary of a category can alter the interpretation of data significantly. How the evaluator anticipates the effects of the program will be manifested has an impact on the type of data collected, the length of time the collection goes on, and the intervals at which the data will be collected. Collecting data in their rawest, noncategorical form allows for more flexibility in the analysis.

KEY TERMS

categorical data	lagged effects
causation	necessary
continuous data	necessary and sufficient
continuous effects	permanency of effects
discontinuous effects	spectacular causes
false negative conclusion	spectacular effects
false positive conclusion	sufficient
intervening variable	targets (benchmarks)

DISCUSSION QUESTIONS

1. Discuss the difference between statistics and causation. Why is it necessary for evaluators to deal with causation?

2. Create your own example of how changing the boundaries of categories using the same raw data can significantly alter your conclusions.

3. Can you think of examples of a lagged effect? A continuous effect? A discontinuous effect? An immediate effect?

CHAPTER

5

THE PRISMS OF VALIDITY

LEARNING OBJECTIVES

After reading this chapter, you should be able to

- Define "threats to validity"
- Understand the four types of validity
- Describe the common threats to each type of validity and how to best minimize or negate them

When planning an evaluation or reading an evaluation report, consider the strength of the research through four related but distinct prisms. These prisms are known as the four types of validity. Validity refers to the extent to which there has been an approximation of truth—if the research is valid in all respects, then the conclusions that are reached through it are legitimate, valid, and generalizable.

In their seminal 1979 book, *Quasi-Experimentation: Design and Analysis Issues for Field Settings,* Cook and Campbell distinguished four types of validity: construct validity, internal validity, statistical conclusion validity, and external validity. This chapter discusses each type of validity and its common threats in the context of program evaluation. Threats to validity are events or circumstances that have the potential to invalidate evaluation research in a certain respect. There may not be anything that the evaluator can do to avoid the threat, but she should be aware that the threat exists and may potentially jeopardize the evaluation, perhaps in an immeasurable way. Other times, though, the threat to validity is so serious that the study's conclusions are not valid—for example, evaluators cannot claim that theoretical constructs have been operationalized appropriately, that the intervention has produced results, or that the results obtained are not simply an anomaly, but are generalizable to other populations.

The best evaluations take threats into account and have been structured to minimize the threats. Because of the real-world constraints on research, evaluators often make trade-offs between types of threats to validity. An evaluator may introduce a less serious threat to validity to the research in order to reduce or avoid a more serious threat.

Ultimately, the goal is to find the evaluation design that is the most robust to threats to validity. You need to learn the threats to validity to plan the best evaluation possible. Threats directly relate to the issue of causation and the choice of the quasi-experimental design (presented in the next chapter). Once one knows which threats to validity are present and need to be balanced, it usually becomes fairly obvious which quasi-experimental designs are applicable and which is the best, given the circumstances.

In brief, **construct validity** refers to the degree to which the theoretical constructs have been well specified, and both the cause and effect constructs have been appropriately operationalized. **Internal validity** pertains to the degree to which the study has shown that a causal relationship exists. **Statistical conclusion validity** refers to the appropriateness of the statistical techniques used for the analysis, and **external validity** refers to the generalizability of the relationship found in one evaluation or study to other people, places, and contexts.

In general, the priority evaluators would give to the types of validity is internal, construct, statistical conclusion, and then external. Certainly, if a relationship has not been shown to exist, there is no reason to generalize the relationship. However, priority between the types of validity may be re-ordered, depending on the reasons for evaluation. For example, if the evaluation is being done to better understand theories behind human behavior (rather than to understand if particular interventions have intended consequences), then the priority might be construct, internal, external, statistical conclusion.

There are more possible threats to each type of validity than discussed here. Those threats are well explicated in Chapter Two of Cook and Campbell's *Quasi-Experimentation.* I discuss here only those that have actually surfaced in my evaluation experience.

Beyond program description issues, there are four sets of questions about a program's causal impact that need to be answered:

■ Is there a relationship between the intervention and the observed outcome? Is program participation related to observed outcome measures?

■ Given that there is a relationship, is this relationship causal? Did the program *cause* the outcome measure to change?

■ Given that the relationship is plausibly causal, what are the particular cause and effect constructs involved in the relationship? What causal construct does the program represent? What effect construct does the outcome measure represent?

■ Given that there is probably a causal relationship between the cause and effect constructs, how generalizable is this relationship across other types of people, other settings, and time periods?

Each set of questions pertains to a type of validity. The first set pertains to statistical conclusion validity, the second set to internal validity, the third set to construct validity, and the fourth set to external validity.

STATISTICAL CONCLUSION VALIDITY

Quantitative analyses are often conducted to determine whether a presumed cause and effect covary. In the simplest form, the cause and effect could either positively or negatively covary. If they positively covary, than an increase in the cause would be associated with an increase in the effect. Conversely, if they negatively covary, then an increase in the cause would be associated with an observed decrease in the effect, and vice versa.

The existence of a covarying relationship does not imply a one-to-one relationship between the causal variable and the effect variable. Covarying relationships can have different strengths. Some may positively covary, but weakly, meaning that an increase in the causal variable is associated with a very small increase in the effect variable. In other relationships, you may find a situation where a slight increase in the causal variable is associated with a very large increase in the effect variable. Or, the relationship may be one where the covariance is found only in a small minority of cases, but in that small minority the impact seems substantial.

Three groups of questions, posed by Cook and Campbell (1979, p. 39), are at the heart of statistical conclusion validity:

1. Is the study designed so that it can detect covariation between the intervention and outcomes? Does the sample size available for study allow for the sensible

use of statistical analysis? You may not be able to draw conclusions about the strength of the statistical relationship if the number of cases available to study is too small to apply appropriate statistical techniques.

2. If covariation can be detected, then does any evidence exist that suggests that the cause and effect actually do covary? If so, what type of evidence exists? Is it anecdotal, or can data be collected and organized so that statistical analyses are appropriate?

3. If there is evidence, how strongly do the intervention and outcomes covary? Will there always be a change in outcome for those who have been touched by the intervention, or will the change in outcomes only be present among some participants? Will there be a large or a small change? How much of the intervention (intensity) does a participant need to receive in order to see a change? Does the intervention work for everybody, or do pre-existing conditions need to exist?

There are two types of errors one can make about the nature of the relationship between the program and its outcomes:

■   **Type I error** occurs when you conclude that the outcomes of the various treatment groups differ, when in reality, they do not. In this case, you erroneously conclude that the program had an impact.

■   **Type II error** occurs when you conclude that the outcomes of the various treatment groups do not differ, when in fact, they do. In this case, you erroneously conclude that the program did not have an impact.

Take a situation where the evaluator concluded that the program is effective—but in fact, the program is ineffective. This evaluator would be making a Type I error. The converse can also occur, where the evaluator concludes that the program has no effect, when in fact, it does. If an erroneous conclusion of no impact has been made, then a Type II error has occurred. A Type I error can result in funding ineffective programs; a Type II error can result in missing opportunities to change behaviors.

When the following situations occur, there is a higher chance of making either a Type I or Type II error. These situations are known as *threats to statistical conclusion validity.*

Small Sample Sizes

Small sample sizes are associated with an increase in the amount of variance around a statistic. The smaller the sample, the larger the variance. Until the sample size hits a minimum of approximately fifty units, the statistic may be too unreliable and real relationships cannot be statistically detected. Thus, the small sample size has introduced a threat to the statistical validity of the evaluation.

Small sample sizes occur in a few ways. Sometimes, programs serve a small number of clients at a time. For example, at a given time, a local child-care center serves a total of thirty-one children across four different age categories—infants, toddlers, early preschool, and late preschool. Clearly, especially when broken down by age category, this number is too small to yield reliable statistics.

One typical approach to increasing the sample size is to combine client data from a number of time periods. For example, rather than only examining data on the thirty-one children in a child-care center in a year, one might combine the data from children in the center this year, last year, and the previous year. If the center serves thirty-one children per year, then the number of children whose data one can analyze increases to ninety-three, a sample size that could allow for many types of statistical analyses. However, if this sample was broken down by age category, it is likely to be too small to avoid the threat to statistical validity.

However, it is important to be careful when combining data across time periods. Combining data is reasonable only when the program and the circumstances of the program have not changed during the period. If changes have occurred, then it would be inappropriate to combine different time periods. Therefore, combine data across different time periods only when both the program and the program's environment have been stable.

Another way that small sample size becomes an issue is when breaking the sample down into smaller groups. Often, it is desirable to see the intervention's effects on men versus women, or on an urban population versus suburban and rural populations, or on various racial or ethnic groups, or on various marital statuses. Even if disaggregating by gender and using a sample of one hundred, then the sample could break down to approximately fifty men and fifty women. When doing analyses on smaller categories, the sample size in each of the cells will decrease even more. In this case, we started with a reasonable sample size, but the answers that we wanted involved breaking the sample down into finer categories with smaller sample sizes. If you can anticipate needing to disaggregate data, then you need to increase the initial sample size to a number that will allow such analysis.

Returning to the child-care center example, let us assume that combining the most recent two years of data is reasonable, but because of programmatic and staffing changes, including data from more than two years ago is inappropriate. This leaves us with a sample of sixty-two children. For many questions involving children, one would disaggregate analyses by age groups. In this sample of sixty-two children, we have sixteen infants (two classes each with eight infants), twenty toddlers (two classes each with ten toddlers), and twenty-six three- and four-year-olds (two classes each with thirteen children). These are very small sample sizes once disaggregated by age. It may not make sense to report "outcomes" because the statistics may vary from year to year—different children will be in the classes at any given time, there may be idiosyncrasies in data collection, and so on.

Another way that small sample size often results is when a sample is taken from a larger population. A researcher may have anticipated a survey response rate that was higher than that achieved, with a resulting sample that is relatively small. One solution to this situation would be to take another sample, and survey this newly selected sample. However, having survey responses from two different points in time might be an issue.

Further, the opportunity to take another sample may not exist. For example, one may plan on surveying one hundred randomly selected "graduates" from a program that served four hundred people, but it's possible that only forty will respond to the survey (a 40 percent response rate). This sample may be too small to provide statistical reliability.

To avoid this situation, you can create a larger sample to begin with, or alternatively, take initial actions that will increase the response rate. Between these two alternatives, the latter is the better approach. It is best to avoid low response rates, because the people who respond to the survey may be systematically different from those who did not respond. Differences between the respondents and nonrespondents could result in a biased sample. Unless you know something about the nonrespondents with respect to how they would have responded to the survey, the respondents may be biased in an unknown way. If you draw conclusions about the program based only on respondents' survey responses, then you may present a skewed picture of the program and its effectiveness. An approach to deal with this situation is to take a small sample of survey nonrespondents, and then continue to follow up with them until they ultimately respond. This is known as sampling for nonresponse follow-up; this sample represents all nonrespondents. One could examine whether the responses of the respondents and the very limited sample of nonrespondents differ.

Creating a survey situation that will result in a higher response rate will reduce potential bias in the surveyed population. Techniques known to increase response rates include: giving people notice of a survey or interview; having someone whom the sampled person respects encourage him to participate in the survey; keeping the survey as short as possible; pretesting the survey instrument; providing respondents with information on the sponsorship of the survey and assurances of confidentiality and anonymity (if appropriate); and incentivizing response.

Incentivizing response often decreases differences between respondents and nonrespondents. For example, giving people cash, checks, or vouchers in exchange for their responses helps increase the response rate. A modest stipend acknowledges to the respondent that you know that providing information is burdensome. Stipends show that the program project respects the respondent's time. Whenever possible, those who are collecting data should offer modest incentives to respondents (for example, grocery store gift certificates).

Measurement Error

Measurement error presents another threat to statistical conclusion validity. Most measures have a degree of imprecision, known as measurement error. Such errors can derive from many sources. For example, if survey questions are not written clearly enough to be interpreted identically by all respondents, then respondents will provide different responses, not because their situations differ, but because their interpretations of the questions differ. Questions may inadvertently collect different information across people, depending on respondents' interpretations, increasing the variance of responses.

Unclear Questions

Unclear questions can also bias responses. If respondents tend to interpret the question in a way that would always elicit a response that is too high or too low, then the statistics derived from the question will be biased.

One common way that the variance in responses is increased occurs when respondents are asked about circumstances or feelings that they may have had in the past. The respondents may reply inaccurately, simply because they cannot perfectly recall the past.

Another source of measurement error results when the survey asks respondents about issues that they do not know with precision, such as the birth dates of other family members, or exactly how much they spend on utilities per month. Respondents may "estimate" their response (for example, reporting the first of the month of birth as the birth date, rounding an amount to the nearest ten dollars.)

It is important that data collection tools be precise enough to collect the intended information, but it is also important to consider that every measure may have some degree of inherent error. Measurement error threatens statistical conclusion validity because it increases the variance of a measure. **When the variance of a measure increases, there is a higher risk that one will make a Type II error—erroneously concluding that there is no effect, when there is.**

When evaluating particularly important measures or issues, there are ways to mitigate the threat of low reliability of measures. For very important measures, it could be important not to rely on simply one question to collect information but to ask supplementary questions that either support or refute the first response. For example, if you were asking about whether a program changed participants' knowledge about a subject (such as drug awareness programs, contraception and abstinence programs, training programs, and so on), you would want to have questions that would affirm what that knowledge base is or was. Further, if you ask about attitudes, you might decide to ask supporting questions that would verify that the person actually holds the attitude that she expresses.

Pretesting a survey provides a safeguard against low question reliability. When pretesting, the surveyor does a post-survey interview to ask the respondent about inconsistent responses and how the respondent interpreted those questions. Pretesting and redrafting the survey instrument should continue until the process has worked out all of the kinks in the instrument.

Unreliable Treatment Implementation

Implementing a treatment unreliably poses a serious threat to statistical conclusion validity. When different implementations of treatment occur, then the variance of the treatment increases, further increasing the likelihood of Type II errors. That is, when the treatment is implemented differently across clients, then one is more likely to conclude erroneously that the treatment had no effect, when in fact it did. There is one exception to this. In an instance where a treatment is being implemented more intensely than program administrators understand it to be, an evaluator may mistakenly conclude that the treatment has a larger effect than it would have had it been implemented as intended. Thus, it is vital that the evaluator have a very thorough understanding of the program and exactly what the treatment entails, before collecting data.

Establishing standards as to exactly what a treatment entails, and training staff on these standards, is vitally important to reduce this threat to statistical conclusion validity.

Fishing

A trait of bad research is when a researcher goes "fishing" when doing quantitative data analysis. Fishing can be thought of as throwing all possible variables into an analysis and letting the statistical analyses (be they t-tests, chi-squared tests, regression analysis, and so on) reveal what variables show statistical significance. This is an atheoretical approach to research, as the analyst tries to come up with a hypothesis that explains the statistically significant relationship(s).

This approach to research is backwards. Statistical analyses should investigate the plausibility of the evaluator's hypotheses. The problem with fishing is that it increases the chance of Type I error—incorrectly concluding that covariation exists. The probability of committing Type I error is called the alpha level and is frequently set at .05. A lower alpha means that there is less than a 5 percent chance of Type I error. If a variable is deemed "statistically significant at the .05 level" then the evaluator interprets that there is less than a 5 percent chance that the statement that the independent and dependent variables covary is incorrect.

When an evaluator goes fishing, he performs tests of statistical significance on many variables—more variables than a priori theories. If using a .05 alpha level, there is a 1 in 20 chance that a variable may be deemed statistically significant although the variable does not actually covary with the dependent variable. If using more than twenty variables, it is likely that one of the tests will lead to erroneous conclusions.

The antidote to fishing is to think clearly about why each variable is included in the analysis. The evaluator should have a rationale for each and every variable. If the evaluator does not have a rationale, then the variable should be omitted.

The goal of an analysis is to discover the most parsimonious model that explains patterns found in the data. Including extraneous variables will deter from this goal.

INTERNAL VALIDITY

Internal validity pertains to whether there is a causal relationship between two variables. Ultimately, evaluators would like to know whether the program caused the change. Whereas statistical conclusion validity pertains only to the presence or absence of a relationship, internal validity asks whether the relationship is causal. The following questions come under the purview of internal validity:

■ Did the program cause the change?

■ Without the program, would we have observed a change? Had the program not existed, what would have happened to participants' outcomes?

■ What is the intensity of the intervention necessary for the change to occur?

■ Do other factors help determine whether the causal process occurs?

As discussed in the causation chapter, determining the direction of causation depends on knowing a time sequence of events. Making false positive, and conversely, false negative conclusions is always a risk. Threats to internal validity are common.

Threat of History

The threat of history occurs when an event that could affect the level of the outcome indicator, independent of the program's influence, occurs during the time between the start and end of the program. Take the example of a mammogram awareness program that provides the community with information about the benefits of early detection of breast cancer. Let's say that during the time that the program was operating, Elizabeth Edwards, wife of 2008 Democratic presidential candidate John Edwards, announced that she was diagnosed with breast cancer, which was detected in a mammogram. If the program was operating during the time that her case was publicized, then women may have been more inclined to get mammograms, not because of the program, but because of the information conveyed in the media about breast cancer.

The threat of history occurs when something that would independently exert an influence on the program's outcomes occurs during the program's operation, but outside of the program. The extent to which the outside occurrence influences the outcome measure is unknown, but clearly, the program cannot claim that all of the change in the outcome is due only to the program's activities. The mammogram awareness program cannot claim that all (or even any) of the increase in mammogram rates can be attributed to the program. If the program were replicated at another time (and if the public forgets about the celebrity case), then evaluators would get a better handle on the extent to which this threat of history affected the program outcome.

Examples of the threat of history contaminating evaluation results abound. The 1996 welfare reform measures pressured welfare mothers to find jobs rather than rely on welfare indefinitely. Some pointed to the rise in employment rates of former welfare recipients as evidence that the intervention resulted in the intended effect of getting people off of public assistance and into jobs. Others, though, noted that the very strong U.S. economy in the late 1990s created an unprecedented demand for nearly all workers and that certainly some of the observed increase in employment and decreased reliance on public assistance was due to the strong economy. So, the question becomes to what extent did the strong economy—rather than welfare reform—cause the rise in welfare mothers' employment rate? This argument is essentially about the threat of history.

Threat of Maturation

The threat of maturation pertains to the fact that some participants may have changed in the way that the program intends them to just because time passed. This threat is especially relevant when conducting evaluations of education programs, where one would expect children to become wiser and stronger as they age. Children are likely to improve their literacy and math skills, knowledge base, emotional capacities, and motor skills to some extent as they age, regardless of whether they participated in programs that stressed such skills.

An example of maturation as a threat would be examining a program that aimed to improve students' reading skills in second grade. If one simply examined the change in reading ability between second and third grade and showed that reading test scores improved, this would not be evidence that the program had any effect because of the threat of maturation. One would expect children to become better readers during this period, simply because time has passed.

Another example of the threat of maturation is the argument over whether the reduction of crime rates in the 1990s was due to crime prevention programs or the aging of the population, which reduced the number of people in the age groups most likely to commit crime.

The threat of maturation does not only appear in evaluations of programs that pertain to children (although when dealing with children, you should always be alert to this threat). In the case of a bereavement support program, an evaluator should be alert to the threat of maturation—some who lost loved ones may cope better simply because time has passed since the loved one's death. In programs that aim to stave off the decline in the physical health of the elderly, a program that showed no change in the physical abilities of its clients may actually have been successful. In these cases there is a trajectory over time that exists, and this trajectory in a sense represents "maturation."

Selection

The threat of selection poses the most insidious threat to internal validity. One should be alert to this threat when evaluating any program in which participation is voluntary. When people can choose whether or not to participate in a program, it is likely that those who participate in the program differ in some way from those who do not participate.

Some argue that if we know the dimensions in which participants and nonparticipants differ, then we can statistically "control" for those dimensions and continue to analyze the program's effectiveness. Stanley Lieberson, in his book *Making It Count* (1985), strongly argues that applying statistical controls for the known differences between participants and nonparticipants still does not address the essence of the selection issue. Participants will differ from nonparticipants in exactly the aspects that the program addresses. On the other hand, Nobel Economics Prize winner James Heckman has spent much of his career developing mathematical models to address the threat of selection.

For example, consider job training programs. If the program is voluntary, then one may suspect that the people who participate in the program tend to be the most motivated—those who perceive that they need job training services and have learned how and where to get them. On one hand, nonparticipants may have already been able to transition to other employment and may not be in need of the program. However, on the other hand, nonparticipants may not be as concerned about their careers, and may be less motivated to receive job training. If participants are more motivated than nonparticipants, one would expect that even without the program, those who choose to participate would have better outcomes in the labor market.

Another example is an MBA program in a prestigious university. The admissions process "creams" (takes the best of) the applicant pool. The threat of selection suggests that even if those accepted and rejected into the school attended the same MBA program, those accepted by the program would have better career outcomes than those who were rejected. Thus, when examining, for example, differences in wage rates between alumni of the prestigious university versus those of a less prestigious university, you should question what proportion of the difference in wage rates is accounted for by differences in the quality of education versus differences in the pool of people who attended the universities.

Evaluations of the food stamp program provide another example of the threat of selection. When examining food insecurity rates of food stamp program participants while receiving food stamps versus comparably poor households that do not participate in the program, an evaluator sees that those who participate in the program (and thus are receiving benefits with which to purchase food) are more food insecure than comparably poor people who do not participate in the program. It may be that people who decide to participate in the program are more concerned with food insecurity even before applying, and this aspect led them to participate in the program in the first place.

Not only is selection an independent threat, but it can interact with other threats. For example, the threat of *selection-maturation* appears when program participants and nonparticipants differ a priori with respect to their pace of growth or rate of change. Even if program participants and nonparticipants appeared identical at the time of entry into the program, differences in their rate of maturation suggest that they would have different post-program levels of the indicators of interest, even without the program's intervention.

Program evaluation is flooded with examples of the threat of selection. Antidotes to the threat of selection mostly focus on using random assignment to equalize treatment and control groups. Other antidotes are to use complex statistical techniques to account for selection. However, Lieberson would argue that the selection issue can never be fully accounted for without randomization because, ultimately, voluntary participants differ from nonparticipants in their propensity to achieve the desired outcome.

Mortality

In the evaluation context, mortality refers to subjects dropping out of a program. One can think of the threat of mortality as a special instance of selection. The threat of mortality occurs when those who stay in a program differ from those who dropped out of the program. When evaluating a program, if the evaluator does not consider the threat of mortality, she may incorrectly estimate the program's impact.

For example, consider a program that has a big impact on a subset of participants in the first few sessions, but less of an impact on another subset. The former subset may drop out of the program after the first few sessions because of the initial sessions' success—these dropouts may feel that they do not need the remainder of the program. If an evaluator estimated the impact of the program by defining "participants" as only those who completed the program, then it is likely that she would *underestimate* the impact of the program.

Conversely, some may drop out because they felt that the program wasn't of benefit to them, and indeed, they experienced less program success in the early stages than those who remained with the program. If participants are defined as only those who completed the program, then the evaluator would likely *overestimate* the program's impact.

An evaluator needs to carefully consider what participating in a program means—does it mean enrolling in the program, or does it mean completing the program? Upon which population should we consider the program's impact? A sizable dropout rate may indicate that the program is not working as intended or is ill-conceived. Examining data on dropouts—who they are, how they differ from those who complete the program, why they dropped out—can yield important insights into the program's operations and outcomes.

Testing

Another important and common threat to internal validity is called testing, which can occur when participants are given the same test or asked the same questions multiple times. Respondents' test scores may change not because of a real change in their knowledge base or in their situation, but because of the respondent's familiarity with the test or heightened awareness of his situation.

Preparatory courses for standardized tests provide students with information on the test. Students often are given practice questions aimed to increase test scores, not because experience with these questions will increase students' knowledge of the subject area, but to familiarize them with the types and formats of questions likely to be asked. Preparatory courses also often simulate the test-taking experience, aimed to reduce anxiety during the real testing and thus raise test scores.

Another example involves when evaluators ask people about a situation, or their emotions, repeatedly. For example, the food security measure asks people questions involving their experiences with food shortages in the household and how they have coped with such shortages. The first time a participant is asked such questions she may respond one way. But even if her situation has not changed, the second time the questions are asked she may respond differently because the initial interview sparked further thought about the issues.

The threat of testing can also lead to a decrease in test scores when a new test is introduced. Between 2005 and 2006, third through eighth grade students in the state of New York experienced a precipitous drop in standardized test scores when a new (and reportedly more rigorous) test was introduced. Some of the decrease was because of the increased rigor of the test, but some was due to unfamiliarity with the new test among both students and teachers. Likewise, between 2006 and 2007, the state enjoyed a significant (approximately 10 percent) increase in test scores, some of which was due to familiarity with the test, but some may be due to a real improvement in students' knowledge. Testing is a serious threat whenever an evaluator asks questions repeatedly on knowledge or attitudes. This threat emerges regularly in education, the arts, and political attitudes. The antidote to the threat of testing is to avoid asking the same people the same questions more than once. Strategies include asking the questions first of one subset of individuals, and then the same questions of a different subset of individuals. A weaker antidote is to change the way information is gleaned from the same respondents—that is, asking the questions differently. In the next chapter, I discuss strategies to make this possible.

Statistical Regression

The threat of statistical regression is a worry when a program is offered only to those who have performed exceptionally well or exceptionally badly on a test. What occurs is that if services are provided to the extremes of performers, for example, either the best or the worse on a single test, it is likely that on subsequent tests those who performed well will regress to the mean (see a decrease in their scores) and those who performed badly will also regress to the mean (see improvement in their scores).

The question becomes what proportion of the changes in the test scores is due to the program's impact versus the effect of the threat of testing. If the threat of testing is not taken into account, then the impact of programs aimed to improve the state of those at the positive tail may be underestimated, and conversely, the impact at the negative tail of the distribution may be overestimated.

For example, consider a tutoring program that is offered to children who score in the bottom 10 percent of a mathematics test. In any test score, there is an element of variation. A child may have scored badly because she was not feeling well, was under undue stress, or otherwise had a bad day. Scoring in the bottom 10 percent is atypical for some; the next time they are tested, some will score better simply because they are not having a bad day. If remedial services are offered to the bottom 10 percent, and one looks at the difference between the initial test score and a post-program test score as evidence of the program's success, then one is likely to overestimate the impact of the remedial services simply because there would have been some regression to the mean even without services. That is, one cannot conclude that all (or any) of the difference between the pretest and the posttest is due to the program, as some children would have scored better in the absence of the program. If the evaluator does not account for the threat of statistical regression, he would overestimate the program's effectiveness.

The converse situation is also true. If gifted support is provided to children who do very well on a single test, one may underestimate the impact of such support if considering the difference between the initial test score and a subsequent test score, because some of the children identified as gifted had a high score on the pretest due to an exceptionally good day.

To address the threat of statistical regression, administrators should offer remedial or gifted services not on the basis of one test, but on the basis of a package of information about an individual. This is more likely to assure that the person truly should be categorized in the tail of the distribution and that the test results are not a fluke.

Instrumentation

The threat of instrumentation appears when the means of data collection changes between a pre-intervention and a post-intervention observation and the change in means affects the level of the observation. For example, say I decided to examine aggression among students and I was able to observe classrooms through one-way mirrors. I am interested in whether a program teaching nonaggressive responses to aggression works. Before the program, I observe the classroom, carefully noting the number of times that an aggressive situation has occurred. I train an assistant to collect the post-program data, and she also makes careful notes about aggressive situations in the classroom. The change in the observer, from me to my assistant, can be considered the threat of instrumentation. Unless the assistant interpreted the situations identically as I would, then it is likely that we will both incorrectly estimate the program's impact.

A change in observers is not the only way that the threat of instrumentation appears. This is also relevant when the same observers become more experienced. The observers may become better at identifying and recording nuanced situations. Therefore, some of the differences between the pretest and posttest information should be attributed to the change in observers' experience level.

This can also happen with interviewers who are orally administering written questionnaires. The interviewers may become more experienced over time, and this may lead to surveys that are better and more quickly administered—ultimately resulting in higher response rates. In this case, the posttest sample may differ somewhat from the pretest sample.

The antidote to both of these situations—a change in the staff of interviewers or observers, and a change in the experience level of data collectors—is to thoroughly train all personnel who will collect data. They should be experienced before actual data collection begins, and their data collection techniques should be standardized. The more discretion given to the data collectors, the more likely that the threat of instrumentation will impact findings.

In surveys, the threat of instrumentation comes into play when the survey instrument changes between the pretest and posttest. To avoid the threat of testing, evaluators may be tempted to ask questions differently on the posttest than how they were asked on the pretest. It is important to be aware that the change in question format, or response format, may introduce the threat of instrumentation. To avoid any problems caused by a change in question wording or reordering of survey questions, surveys should be thoroughly pretested before they are used for data collection. All of the possible kinks should be worked out of the survey beforehand.

Diffusion of Treatments

The diffusion of a treatment presents a threat to internal validity because it is not clear whether the group identified to be the control group actually received no treatment. This may ultimately result in an incorrect conclusion that the treatment has no impact, when in fact, it does.

Diffusion of a treatment occurs when the treatment and the control groups overlap. For example, take a billboard campaign that occurred in a low-income neighborhood to encourage residents to take advantage of an energy assistance program. In this program, households in another low-income neighborhood in the same city are used as the control group. The evaluators planned to examine the impact of the billboard campaign by looking at the difference in number of applications for the program originating in the neighborhood where the billboards appeared, versus the number from the other neighborhood. However, this design is valid only to the extent that those in the control neighborhood did not observe the billboards in the other neighborhood. If the billboards appeared on a main thoroughfare that some in the control neighborhood would drive on, then the quasi-experimental design may not be valid because of the threat of the diffusion of treatment.

Another way that diffusion can occur is when the treatment group shares information with the control group. Sharing information is a possibility when the treatment provided is seen as clearly beneficial, as in the case of social service programs, programs that offer monetary benefits, or programs that offer something that is otherwise hard to get. If the control group receives all or part of the treatment unbeknownst to the evaluator, she is likely to underestimate the program's impact.

Compensatory Equalization of Treatments

This threat is a special case of diffusion of treatments that can occur when subjects are randomly assigned to treatment or control groups. If those providing the treatment do not feel comfortable with the random assignment, they may try to provide the control group with either the actual treatment or some version of it. In this sense, they are compensating for the "no treatment" state of subjects in the control group.

For example, consider an organization operating a program that aimed to increase homeownership by walking potential applicants through the homebuying and mortgage processes. One way of determining the effectiveness of the program would be to randomly assign potential homebuyers to the program. However, organization staff may feel uncomfortable with the prospect of not helping other, equally needy people through the homebuying and mortgage process, and on an informal basis, they assist those who are not assigned to the program.

To address the possibility of compensatory equalization of treatments, those administering the treatment-control group design need to understand the research importance of withholding the treatment from the control group. Some staff may not feel comfortable withholding a treatment and may even feel that it is ethically wrong to do so. This is especially the case if the treatment is a desired good. To avoid this situation, there may be more buy-in to the quasi-experimental situation if the control group receives the treatment at a later date, rather than not at all.

Compensatory Rivalry and Resentful Demoralization

These two threats—*compensatory rivalry by respondents receiving less desirable treatments* and *resentful demoralization of respondents receiving less desirable treatments*— occur when those in the control group resent being in the control group. They do one of two things. In the first case, the control group displays the "John Henry" effect, where the group behaves abnormally well to show that they are better than the treatment group. (This is called the "John Henry" effect in reference to the American folk tale about John Henry, the railroad steel-driver who, in a contest with a new steam-powered drill, worked himself to death.)

Conversely, if the control group knows that it isn't receiving the benefits that the treatment group is receiving, the group may perform abnormally worse than it would have had there been no program or if the group was not aware that it was not getting treatment. This is the threat of the resentful demoralization of respondents receiving a less desirable treatment.

In either case, the control group performs abnormally, resulting in an inaccurate estimate of the impact of the treatment. If an evaluator were to estimate the impact of the treatment under these circumstances, he would either over- or underestimate.

Showing that the intervention has the intended impact is the essence of internal validity. In addition to these threats, it is important to consider the causal relationship being proposed and ask whether the evidence supports the proposition of the causal relationship. For this relationship to exist, the cause must come before the effect, and the type and form of the relationship should be considered. Even if an evaluation is not endangered by any of the above internal validity threats, the causal relationship between the program and outcomes may not exist.

More than one internal validity threat can operate in a given situation. Consider the theoretical effects that each of the threats may have on the causal relationship (gross bias), and the net bias that will result from the threats.

Depending on the severity of the threats to internal validity, the causal relationship inferred may or may not be valid. Therefore, evaluators should decide upon a quasi-experimental design that minimizes these threats.

CONSTRUCT VALIDITY

Construct validity pertains to whether theoretical constructs have been operationalized appropriately, the extent to which the relationships observed can be generalized to theoretical constructs, and the extent to which the measures used reflect theoretical constructs. Any relationship between two theoretical constructs ought to be robust, regardless of how the evaluator operationalizes and measures the constructs. Much can be learned from programs that deal with the same theoretical relationships, even if those relationships are not operationalized and measured the same way.

Generally, there are no common definitions of theoretical constructs. These definitions change from study to study, from researcher to researcher, and from context to context. For example, what one person may label an "employability" initiative, another might call a "human capital development" initiative. Evaluators may be hard-pressed when asked for the shared definition of "empowerment," although plenty of programs have the goal of empowerment. Therefore, it is important to be clear about how a construct is defined.

There exist five steps that the evaluator should consider when thinking about construct validity:

1. The evaluator should think through a construct's definition, considering how others have defined the construct and how a lay person would interpret it.

2. The evaluator should consider whether there are other, possibly related constructs from which the construct at hand ought to be differentiated. In these two steps, the evaluator needs to be clear about what the construct is and equally important, what it is not.

3. The evaluator should consider how one would measure the now well-defined construct, first considering measures that have been used by others. Recycling measures is wise for a number of reasons. First, using a measure that others can use enhances the opportunity for direct comparison—for example, comparing outcomes between programs, comparing the state of clients before and after they receive program services. Second, if a measure has been used repeatedly, there may be research on its validity and reliability. For example, common measures, such as using self-reported health status as a measure of health status, have a research history. Evaluators should not waste time reinventing the wheel and should, when possible and appropriate, use predeveloped measures.

4. In the best of all worlds, evaluators should use more than one measure of a construct to assure that only the construct at hand is being measured. I can think of no construct that could be measured in one and only one way. For example, if I use an employment rate as my measure of "labor market success" for a program that intends to improve participants' employability, and this is the only measure used, then regardless of what happens with the employment rate, I cannot be sure whether what is being measured reflects participants' employability, or simply a change in labor market conditions. If I add on measures such as skills test results, and the ranking of clients to potential employers, then I will be more assured that I have measured "employability" rather than shifts in the economy.

5. Regardless of the measures used, they should be robust to how data on the measure are collected. The measurement of the construct should be robust to

whether data were collected using phone interviews versus internet surveys, observer information versus self-reported, administrative data versus self-reports.

Mono-Operation Bias

The most serious and most common threat to construct validity is called mono-operation bias, which occurs when only one measure is used to reflect a theoretical construct. For example, the theoretical construct C can be operationalized many different ways. For example, consider micro-finance programs targeted at women, through which women are given credit and loans to assist in small business development. The goal of one such program was to improve the well-being of the family. The program theory is that if women are given small loans, they can develop small businesses, thus increasing the women's income and the family's income, ultimately improving the family's overall well-being. The construct of family well-being can be considered many different ways—housing stock, health status of family members, access to clean water, education, and so on. If evaluators chose only one way of measuring family well-being—for example, disease rates of family members—they would not be sure that they were measuring family well-being or another construct, such as community health (which could be affected, for instance, by World Health Organization vaccination campaigns). But if they add more measures, such as whether children attend school and levels of domestic violence, they become more assured that they are actually measuring family well-being. Operationalizing the construct in all possible ways allows you to be assured that the construct of family well-being is being affected, and not the construct of community health.

Mono-operation bias is more of a threat in program evaluation when examining cause rather than effect. When evaluating programs, the causal construct is usually operationalized one way—by the program itself. Therefore, the program's activities are the operationalization of the causal construct, and thus the causal construct is usually operationalized in only one way.

There are usually opportunities to design the measurement of the effect construct so that it has strong construct validity. Many different aspects of this construct can be considered and incorporated into the design of measurement systems.

Mono-Method Bias

Another threat to construct validity, mono-method bias occurs when the various measurements are presented in the same way. For example, one may be considering different aspects of the construct in a survey, and asking respondents to scale the degree to which they agree with a series of statements. Each statement considers different aspects of the construct, but the respondent is given a litany of statements. This type of survey has low construct validity because it is not certain that the respondent actually thought about the question, or whether an answer to one question affects answers to another.

Construct validity becomes important when deciding which literature to review. Evaluators review literature for many reasons, including to find support for the hypothesis of a causal relationship between theoretical constructs. If you restrict the literature review only to those programs that look exactly like the program being evaluated, then typically, the literature review would be quite short. However, the relevant literature isn't only studies that have considered similar programs, and it is worthwhile to review the literature on causal relationships between the theoretical constructs.

For example, if my labor skills program, which enhances participant's computer skills, is intended to lead to jobs for participants, and if the computer skills program is an operationalization of the causal construct of "better skills," and if "jobs for participants" is an operationalization of the effect construct of "better labor market outcomes," then the literature reviewed should include other programs that aim to improve labor market outcomes by enhancing participants' skills through other avenues. For example, the evaluator would review programs that provide training in other ways, such as programs that aim to increase workers' job retention by boosting their mechanical skills, because such a program pertains to both the causal and effect constructs of interest. Any study involving the theoretical constructs of interest should be reviewed to provide evidence that the theoretical relationship that the designers of the program believe exists has been found to exist in other situations. Whether those studies showing the theoretically posited relationship are likely to apply to the situation at hand is an issue of external validity.

EXTERNAL VALIDITY

External validity deals with the appropriateness of generalizing findings from one study to other settings, places, times, and types of people. Even if a strong causal relationship was shown to exist between a program and outcomes in one instance, that does not mean that this relationship between the program and outcomes will exist if the program is replicated elsewhere. There are many reasons why evaluators may not be able to replicate findings.

Different time periods. If a relationship is found at one point in time, the relationship may not be found at another point in time; this is called "period effects." Circumstances, beliefs, politics, culture, and social mores change with time. A study that found even an identical program effective some time ago may have questionable external validity simply because of the passage of time.

It is impossible to determine how much time must pass for a study to become obsolete. Sometimes, things are slow to change, and at other times, rapid change can occur. For example, depending on the topic, an evaluator might have felt comfortable in the later 1990s relying on a study that was done in the 1980s, when both periods were experiencing economic expansion. However, if the economic scene is important, then one might not want to use studies conducted during times of great prosperity if the current period is one of economic decline.

Different places. Studies on a program conducted in one locale may not apply to another locale because they present different challenges. A locale may have a unique history, which makes generalizing findings from it or to it inappropriate. When considering whether past studies on other locales apply to a specific program's locale, it is wise to consider whether the locales have a similar history and present similar challenges. For example, a program that works in an urban area may not be equally as effective in a suburban or rural area—population density may be needed for the program to be effective. Also, programs conducted in one country may show different rates of success in other countries.

When considering the history of a locale, evaluators should consider how systems have evolved over time, and even how the society tends to think about certain issues. For example, New Englanders are famous for their sense of individualism, and Pittsburgh is known for playing a pivotal role in U.S. labor history. Daponte and Bade conducted a study (2000) comparing the strength of the private food assistance network (such as food pantries and food banks) in Pittsburgh, Pennsylvania, and Bridgeport, Connecticut, concluding that the way in which each locale thought about the problem of domestic hunger and solutions to it influenced how each city's private food assistance network evolved. Pittsburgh's response to domestic hunger was much stronger than that found in Bridgeport. Thus, we would not expect studies on domestic hunger in Pittsburgh or anywhere in Pennsylvania to apply equally well to Connecticut, and perhaps such differences would weaken the external validity of studies conducted on programs in areas that have a strong sense of class-consciousness to any area where individualistic responses are paramount.

Not only may different areas have differing past histories, but the areas may also have observably dissimilar types of populations. Observable differences are generally thought of as those in demographic characteristics, such as age, gender, race or ethnicity, educational attainment, and socioeconomic status. Studies done on males may not apply equally well to females, and studies done on a population with low educational attainment may not apply equally well to a population with high educational attainment.

Thus, when reviewing literature and applying results of studies to the population at hand, evaluators should consider to what degree, if any, the findings from an evaluation can be generalized to the population at hand. You should ultimately reflect on these questions:

- Has a length of time passed that might make the study weak in external validity?

- Was the study done on a specific or a broad population?

- Were analyses done separately on subpopulations? If so, was the relationship found consistent among subpopulations?

- In what setting was the program operating? Is there a difference between that setting and the one currently being studied?

- Is there anything unique about the intervention being reviewed that might set it apart from other attempts at the same intervention? For example, the intervention may have had uniquely trained staff or headed by a director who had unique experience or community connections.

If the answer to all of these questions suggests that there is no reason, a priori, to suspect that the findings may not have external validity, then you would rely more on those findings than on a set of findings that do not have external validity.

To increase an evaluation's external validity, evaluators would examine an intervention's impact not only on the entire population, but on subpopulations. For example, you would ask: Does the intervention have the same impact on people of different educational levels? Different ages? Different ethnicities? Different genders? Different sexual orientations? Who live in different areas? If no differences appear by subcategory, then you would conclude that the intervention's effects are relatively robust to the particular population in which it occurred. If there appear to be differences, though, then you would begin to doubt whether the results are externally valid across times, settings, and populations.

All four types of validity speak to the strength of a study and its theoretical usefulness. In designing an evaluation, evaluators would want to use a design that is the strongest possible in all four ways, but this may not always be possible. The next chapter discusses which quasi-experimental designs to use in order to maximize the validity of an evaluation.

SUMMARY

There are four types of validity through which research should be considered: statistical conclusion validity, internal validity, construct validity, and external validity. Threats to validity are events or circumstances that can potentially invalidate research in a certain respect. The best evaluations take into account these threats and are structured to minimize them.

KEY TERMS

compensatory equalization	resentful demoralization
compensatory rivalry	small sample size
construct validity	statistical conclusion validity
diffusion of a treatment	threat of history
external validity	threat of instrumentation
fishing	threat of maturation
internal validity	threat of mortality
measurement error	threat of selection
mono-method bias	threat of statistical regression
mono-operation bias	threat of testing
negatively covary	threats to validity
observable differences	type I error
period effects	type II error
positively covary	validity

DISCUSSION QUESTIONS

1. In general, why is internal validity the most important type in evaluation studies?

2. Choose an example from the end of Chapter Two. Can you answer the four questions about a program's causal impact? What threats to validity would you be most concerned with? How would you try to minimize those threats?

CHAPTER

6

ATTRIBUTING OUTCOMES TO THE PROGRAM

Quasi-Experimental Design

LEARNING OBJECTIVES

After reading this chapter, you should be able to

- Understand the needs and limitations of different quasi-experimental designs
- Be able to diagram quasi-experimental designs

The ultimate goal of a program or intervention is to effect change. Attributing changes to the intervention presents the ultimate challenge to evaluators.

Quasi-experimental design allows evaluators to think about the outcomes in a structured way. Which quasi-experimental design you choose determines the timing of the outcome observations collected for the attribution of change.

You should not confuse quasi-experimental design with the quantitative analysis of data, as even qualitative data analysis requires that the structure of data collection ultimately allow for causal attribution. Although you can use quantitative methods to statistically show the level and statistical significance of the change, quasi-experimental design is used to determine the timing and structure of data collection, thus should be used when collecting qualitative data.

Quasi-experimental design informs the question of what we would have expected to occur in the treatment group without the intervention. This chapter introduces and discusses a number of quasi-experimental designs that were put forth by Cook and Campbell (1979), starting with the simplest cases where causation cannot be shown, to more complex and robust designs. It is best to use the design that minimizes threats to validity. The design ultimately used for a given intervention will be based on a decision that weighs the different types of validity and the different threats to each of the validity types. You should select a design that makes the best use of the situation at hand.

QUASI-EXPERIMENTAL NOTATION

To display the quasi-experimental designs, we use the notation used by Cook and Campbell. "O" indicates an observation, and "X" indicates the intervention or treatment. Numerical subscripts indicate the first, second, third (and so on) observations, and lettered subscripts indicate a different type of observation or treatment. The design should be read from left to right, and rows separated by dotted lines indicate non-equivalent groups.

Here, we continue Cook and Campbell's tradition of naming the designs, although in practice, evaluators usually communicate about the designs by sketching out the design, not by the formal name of the design.

Sketching out the chosen design clarifies which design the evaluation will use as well as the threats to validity that the design does and does not address. Knowing the designs and their associated threats to validity are part of the set of tools evaluators bring to the table. Evaluators should be well versed in quasi-experimental design.

The actual observations of the quasi-experimental design are the outcomes specified in the program logic model. The outcome measures inform what one will observe and keep track of; the quasi-experimental design informs how the outcomes will be used to show that the change in the outcome is attributable to the program.

An evaluator may use more than one quasi-experimental design when evaluating a program, although typically, the same design is used with different outcomes being examined. However, there can be situations where different outcomes present another opportunity, or different types of outcomes may be particularly vulnerable to a specific threat to validity. We start by considering designs that typically cannot be used to prove a causal relationship between the program and its outcomes.

FREQUENTLY USED DESIGNS THAT DO NOT SHOW CAUSATION

One-Group Posttest-Only

In this design (Cook and Campbell, 1979, p. 96), only the outcomes of the treatment group (which consists only of program participants) are examined and only at one point in time—after the program. Nonparticipants of the program are never examined.

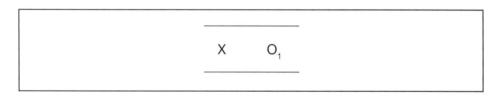

Source: Cook and Campbell (1979), p. 96.

Evaluators cannot comment on the change that occurred to the treatment group because pre-treatment information about the group is not known. Further, you cannot comment on what a comparable group would have done in the absence of the treatment, because a comparable group is not examined.

All threats to internal validity apply to this design. Causation cannot be shown because one cannot even say that a change in the outcome occurred. Even if the posttest shows that the treatment group had a "good outcome," one doesn't know whether the outcome changed over time or even the level of the "outcome" for a comparable group of people.

Needless to say, this design should never be used. No change can be shown to have occurred. Unfortunately, use of this design is not uncommon. I have seen many programs that use this design in situations where data collection was an afterthought. The programs believe that if they can show that their participants have good outcomes, then the programs must have been successful. This thinking is erroneous because not only does this design not indicate that any change occurred, it cannot show that the program caused the change to occur.

Posttest-Only with Nonequivalent Groups

A variation on the prior design is to add a control group, which is technically known as a "nonequivalent" group because the treatment and control groups do not draw from the same population. The two groups differ in ways that are sometimes observable (for example, demographic traits) and sometimes nonobservable (such as motivation or willingness to participate in the program).

$$X \qquad O_1$$
$$\text{-----------------------}$$
$$O_1$$

Source: Cook and Campbell (1979), p. 98.

For example, take two people who look identical with respect to every observable characteristic imaginable—they live in the same neighborhood, are the same age, are of the same race or ethnicity, speak the same language, live in the same family structure, have the same number of children, same socioeconomic status, same education, and so on. These two people can still differ in their propensity to participate in the program; this difference is an unobservable characteristic. So, even when comparing the treatment and control groups, you are comparing two nonequivalent groups.

In this posttest-only design, illustrated in Cook and Campbell (p. 98), the evaluator does not know how these groups differed with respect to the outcome measure(s) of interest even before the program began. Although all threats to validity apply, probably the most severe threat to this design is selection, a threat to internal validity. The groups could have differed in terms of their outcome measures prior to the program's start, or their rate of change in the outcome measure, but the evaluator would not have such information. Consider a program that provided incentives for low-income people to save for certain expenses, such as education and purchasing a first home. Those most likely to save may be more likely to participate in the program. Even if the outcome measure of the amount of money saved was shown to be higher among program participants than nonparticipants, you could not conclude that the program caused that change—because of the threat of selection. Those who participate in the program may have been more prone to saving in the first place. Therefore, the causal statement could not be made.

Sometimes, a variation of this design is used where, rather than considering one treatment group as compared to a control group, the treatment instead is provided in varying intensities. This design only makes sense when you would expect different intensities of the treatment to yield proportionately different outcome—the degree of change would depend on the treatment's intensity.

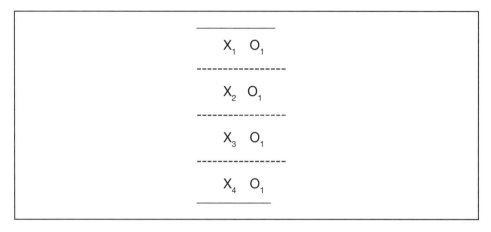

$$X_1 \quad O_1$$

$$X_2 \quad O_1$$

$$X_3 \quad O_1$$

$$X_4 \quad O_1$$

Source: Cook and Campbell (1979), p. 99.

In this design, whether causation can be shown depends on how participants were assigned to each of the groups receiving varying intensities of treatment. If the participants themselves choose the intensity, then causation cannot be shown because of the threat of selection. However, if participants are entered into the program and then program administrators **randomly assign** participants to one of the categories of intensity of treatment, then evaluators may be able to make a credible statement along the lines of "among people who desire the program, when the program is provided in a more intense manner, the participants experience a greater change in their outcomes than they do when the program is provided less intensely." In order for this statement to have any credibility, though, random assignment must have occurred after participants availed themselves of some form of the program.

Participants' Pretest-Posttest

Another frequently used design that does not provide causation compares a single pretest with a single posttest measure of only the treatment group. Often, programs either do not have access to a reasonable control group or have not pursued control group data. However, the program does have ability to collect data from its participants. In this design, the program records participants' outcome measure(s) at the time of entry into the program and again after the program's termination. If participants' outcome

$$O_1 \quad X \quad O_2$$

Source: Cook and Campbell (1979), p. 99.

measures improved, then the program was successful. Most programs that use this design assume that if the outcome measure(s) changed, then the program caused the change to occur.

This design is vulnerable to all of the threats to internal validity. For example, the threat of maturation could pertain because the participants may have been on a trajectory where their outcomes would have improved in time even without the intervention. If a "test" were used, the test scores between the first and second observation of the outcome measure could increase, because of the threat of testing. The lack of a control group does not allow one to infer the degree to which the measure has increased because of testing.

The threat of history would pertain if an event occurred outside of the program that would have influenced the participants' outcome measures. The threat of statistical regression could appear with this design if the participants were chosen from either tail of a distribution.

DESIGNS THAT GENERALLY PERMIT CAUSAL INFERENCES

Untreated Control Group Design with Pretest and Posttest

This design, the most basic that permits causal inference, includes both a treatment and a control group and two observations—one pretreatment and one posttreatment. The first observation, O_1, refers to the same point in time in both the treatment and control groups, as does O_2.

$$O_1 \quad X \quad O_2$$
$$\text{-----------------------}$$
$$O_1 \qquad\quad O_2$$

Source: Cook and Campbell (1979), p. 104.

The first observation, which occurs before the treatment group receives the program's benefits, is recorded to determine the degree to which the treatment and control groups vary in the outcome even before completing the program. If the pretreatment measures are identical or nearly so, despite nonequivalence between the treatment and control groups, an evaluator would feel more comfortable using the control group as a control.

The timing of the second observation is critically important. Because the design only examines the observations at two points in time, there is scant evidence to prove causation. The challenge is to collect the second observation when the program has had its effect. But if the program produces a lagged effect and you collect the second observation too early, the program will appear ineffective even if eventually it has a substantial impact on participants.

The converse is also true. If the program's effects are only short-lived and dissipate over time, collecting the second observation too early will make the program seem effective, when in fact it is only temporarily effective. For example, if one were examining weight-loss programs and the second observation was collected at the time of the program's completion, evaluators may find that program participants lost 10 percent of their body weight while nonparticipants did not lose any weight—and conclude that the program was effective. However, if the second observation was based on weight one year after the program's completion, evaluators may instead find no difference between participants and nonparticipants. That is, even though the program's true effect was temporary weight loss, collecting the data too early made the program look more effective than it was and collecting the data too late makes the program appear that it had neither a short-term nor a long-term effect on weight loss.

Also, because the posttest is only a single data point, you cannot determine the function that the effect may take. Some effects may cause a sudden one-time change after which participants revert back to their typical growth pattern (a change in intercept). Another effect may be a change in the growth rate (a change in slope). With only two data points, you cannot distinguish which type of effect occurred—you also cannot comment on whether the effect is likely to persist (a continuous effect) or whether participants are likely to return back to their pre-treatment levels (non-continuous effect). To some degree, how one interprets outcomes from this design depends on the particular pattern of outcomes. There are four patterns to consider.

Pattern 1 Consider a situation where the control group experienced no change between pretest and posttest in its outcome measures—that is, for the control group, $O_1 = O_2$. The treatment group shows an increase in its outcome, $O_2 > O_1$ (Figure 6.1).

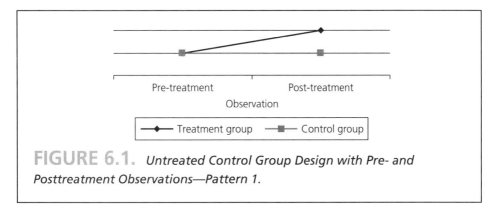

FIGURE 6.1. *Untreated Control Group Design with Pre- and Posttreatment Observations—Pattern 1.*

Source: Cook and Campbell (1979), p. 105.

If the control group is comparable to the treatment group, then you would assume that observing no change in the control group's outcome(s) supports the argument that the threats of maturation and testing do not apply. You would interpret the stability of the control group's observations as evidence that natural growth would have caused no change in the treatment group's observations, and also that repetition of the test had no effect on test scores. With respect to maturation, you would really want to know more about the group's rate of growth prior to the treatment group's participation in the program, by examining more pre-treatment observations of both groups.

If the observations were collected identically between the treatment and control groups, you would not be able to explain the change in the observations of the treatment as an effect of instrumentation because the control group's observations were also exposed to this threat. Also, if there was no unique "historical" event that would have contaminated the treatment group, then the threat of history also would not apply. If there was a "historical" event that might have contaminated the change in observations, but both the treatment and control groups experienced that event, then the design negated the threat of history.

Selection could be a threat depending on exactly how you created the groups. In an instance in which the people in the treatment and control groups were aware of the treatment's availability, the treatment group desired the treatment enough to participate and the control group did not desire the program and decided not to participate. The control group may have felt no need for the treatment or may have received the treatment elsewhere. In this instance, the control and treatment groups differ in a fundamental way—their desire to receive the treatment—and the difference in their desire for the treatment could correlate with their respective outcome measures.

On the other hand, the control group may have had no awareness of the treatment. If the members of the treatment group were aware of the treatment and the members of the control group were unaware of the treatment, you need to consider whether the reasons that the two groups differ in their awareness could affect any difference in their outcomes. If treatment awareness is correlated with the outcome measure, then some of the difference of the post-treatment outcome measures is attributable to the sorting of people into treatment and control groups based not only on the respective desirability of the treatment to the two groups, but also on their awareness of the treatment.

What if the control group is composed of those not eligible for the program? Whether the control group is comparable to the treatment group will depend on the eligibility criteria. For example, eligibility criteria such as income are likely to have some independent effect on many outcome measures. However, if the program is offered only to people in a certain neighborhood and there are comparable geographic areas that are not eligible for the program, then the non-eligible control group may be a reasonable comparison.

If participants were randomly assigned to the treatment or control groups and the pre-treatment measures appeared similar between the groups, then the random assignment will remove the threat of selection. Random assignment using this simple design can be difficult to structure because of ethical issues and the general unwillingness of an untreated control group to provide data. This design requires two data points from the control group—the group that never receives any of the program's benefits. People in the control group may be reluctant to provide information to the program when they are not receiving the potential benefits.

It may be unethical to withhold benefits from the control group and yet collect information from them. If the program is clearly beneficial or has a high likelihood of being so, ethical limitations may prevent evaluators from even having a control group. I have found that many nonprofits are understandably reluctant to form no-treatment control groups for research purposes. The next design, the delayed treatment design, overcomes these ethical issues in most cases.

Pattern 2 In the second type of pattern that can emerge, the treatment group has a higher pretest score than the control group, and the treatment group shows a greater increase in outcome between the first and second observations than does the control group (Figure 6.2). The risk here is interpreting this pattern as evidence that the treatment was effective.

This pattern is very common when people self-select the treatment group. The issue is the degree to which the groups were nonequivalent at the start in terms of their rates of growth or maturation. That is, a selection-maturation effect, where those who selected themselves for the program would have had a higher rate of growth even in the program's absence, makes it appear that the program is effective when in fact it may not be.

One example of this could be when comparing the test scores of children going to magnet versus nonmagnet schools. It may seem that the magnet school is producing a

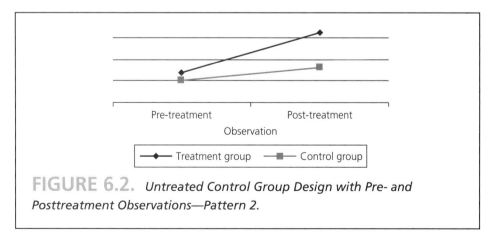

FIGURE 6.2. *Untreated Control Group Design with Pre- and Posttreatment Observations—Pattern 2.*

Source: Cook and Campbell (1979), p. 106.

steeper rise in knowledge. However, it may be that parents who are in the know about educational opportunities and take advantage of them have children who score better on tests, or who take education more seriously. It may be that the magnet school has no effect other than sorting children on the basis of parents' awareness of better educational opportunities for their children.

Pattern 3 Another pattern can occur when the control group's pretest score exceeds that of the treatment group, and the control group shows no change in scores between the two time periods although the treatment group experienced a positive increase in scores (Figure 6.3). This result is likely when there is an incentive for the treatment group's performance to improve. If such an incentive exists and is not part of the program, then the improvement should not be confused with true program effectiveness.

Pattern 3 could result when there is a "ceiling" on a test. It could be that the control group did not show an improvement on the test because it is not possible to show this based on the way the outcome is measured. For example, if the top income category is $75,000 and over, and the control group's mean income rose from $76,000 to $106,000, although there was a $30,000 real increase, the data would not show it because of ceiling effects. The treatment group, with its lower income would be able to show changes because it had not yet reached the ceiling of the data collection instrument.

Statistical regression is another threat to internal validity to be considered when using this design. If the treatment group was composed of people who did particularly poorly on a pretest, it is likely that their scores would have regressed to the mean in any case.

However, this design rules out the threat of selection-maturation. Usually, people who score low on the pretest are likely to have slower outcome growth rates than those

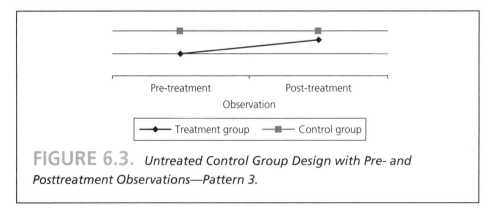

FIGURE 6.3. *Untreated Control Group Design with Pre- and Posttreatment Observations—Pattern 3.*

Source: Cook and Campbell (1979), p. 110.

who had higher pretest scores. If between the first and second observations the initially low-scoring treatment group shows a higher rate of growth than the higher scoring control group, it is likely that the treatment was so successful that the treatment group overcame the expectation that it would have been even further behind the control group in the posttest.

Pattern 4 This pattern is similar to the third pattern, but at posttest, the treatment group scores even higher than the control group (Figure 6.4). This outcome is the most desirable. In such a case, the program was offered to those who did not score as well in the pretest, and then had better outcomes than the untreated control group.

Because the second observation is even higher than that of the control group, a ceiling effect could not be operating. Although a ceiling effect can explain why a low-scoring pretest group could score as high as the higher-scoring group, it cannot explain the crossover in scores between the two groups.

Also, the threat of regression becomes less likely because of the crossover. This threat, even if very powerful, would cause the treatment group to have scores more similar to those of the control group. However, the threat of regression could not explain a treatment group scoring higher than the control group.

The crossover in the level of the outcome measure(s) also suggests that the threat of selection-maturation does not apply. It is unlikely that the initially low-scoring treatment group would suddenly develop a higher rate of improvement in outcomes than the treatment group.

If the design yields this crossover, the causal statements that derive may seem relatively robust. Using this design in the hopes of achieving this result is a risky strategy. The evaluator is better off using a stronger design when possible.

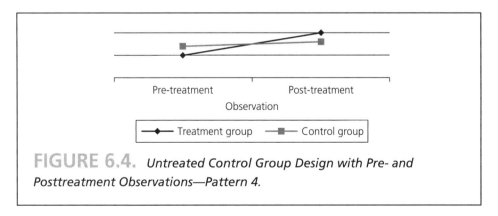

FIGURE 6.4. *Untreated Control Group Design with Pre- and Posttreatment Observations—Pattern 4.*

Source: Cook and Campbell (1979), p. 111.

Delayed Treatment Control Group

I have found that the most useful, palatable, and parsimonious design is one where the control group eventually receives the treatment, but at a later date than the treatment group. This design is sometimes known as the switching replications design.

Early	O_1	X	O_2		O_3
Delayed	O_1		O_2	X	O_3

In this design, three data points are collected from the early treatment group and the control group, which is the delayed treatment group. If you consider only the O_1 and O_2 observations, then the design reduces down to the previous design. That is, O_2 of the delayed group provides information about what O_2 of the early group would have been had the group not received the treatment.

Adding a third observation to the early treatment group provides some, albeit limited, information on how long-lasting the treatment's effects may be.

Between Time 2 and Time 3, the delayed group finally receives the treatment. That both groups receive the treatment allays some of the ethical concerns that non-profit administrators have about no-treatment control groups. Further, the availability of the delayed treatment makes this design palatable to Institutional Review Boards (IRBs) which are the committees in academic settings that review research designs for ethical issues. In U.S. universities, social science research usually needs IRB approval before it can proceed. Nonprofits usually do not have formal IRBs, but are equally concerned about potential ethical violations that research designs may present.

One can argue that with this design, everybody eventually receives the treatment; therefore, ultimately, no one is exploited. The only thing that is being withheld is the timing of the treatment, which may not be an issue at all if the program typically has a waiting list of people who desire the treatment.

The key here is how one allocates participants to the early versus the late treatment groups. If the allocation is done randomly, then the groups should be statistically equivalent. However, if the allocation is done on a first-come, first-serve basis, then the early and delayed treatment groups could differ in unobservable ways. That is, one might argue that the early treatment group is comprised of those more motivated to receive the treatment's benefits than participants in the delayed treatment group, and thus the groups' outcomes may be non-comparable.

The ideal way to carry out this design is for a program first to create a list of everyone interested in participating in the program. Neither group will start the program until this list is compiled. Typically, program administrators would saturate the target population with messages about the program's availability, and then give potential participants time to enroll in the program. When people first contact the program, the staff explains to them that the program will be offered at one of two times and assignment to groups is determined randomly. Data from potential participants are collected when the program screens potential participants using the program's eligibility criteria. Only those found eligible for the program are included on this list. The screening data of the eligible participants should comprise O_1.

Then, everyone on the entire list is divided randomly into two groups—the early and the delayed treatment groups, and each group is informed when it will receive the treatment. The early treatment group goes through the program. When their posttreatment outcome is first measured (O_2), the second pretreatment outcome is measured for the delayed treatment group (O_2). Usually, when the early group completes the program, the delayed group's outcomes will be measured again (O_2). The evaluator should note if there are people who decline to be measured because they no longer need the program. Such cases are important because they suggest that the program was not necessary for participants to experience change in outcome.

The third data point for the early group is a second posttreatment data point and for the delayed group is the first posttreatment data point. The O_2–O_3 change for the delayed group may mimic the early group's O_1–O_2 change. If it does, then you would place more credence on the causal statement that the program produced the effect, because the same relationship was observed in both groups at two different time periods. Thus, the threat of history seems unlikely.

This design was used by Daponte, Sanders, and Taylor (1999) in an experiment conducted on whether informing people of the exact dollar amount for which they are eligible in food stamp benefits affects their food stamp participation rates. To summarize, the experiment was that all of the participants, who were comparably poor and lived in the Pittsburgh, Pennsylvania, metropolitan area, were not using food stamps in the fall of 1993. The researchers randomly divided the sample into two treatment groups—early and delayed. The early group was contacted between January and March 1994, and asked whether they would be willing to be screened for food stamp eligibility if the researchers gave them a $10 food store certificate. Nearly all agreed to be in this experiment. The interviewer screened the participant for food stamp eligibility and informed the participant of the exact dollar amount he would receive in benefits if he were to enroll in the program. Six weeks later, in March, the participants were contacted again for follow-up and asked whether they applied for benefits and if not, why not.

When the follow-up of the early group occurred, the delayed group was screened to determine whether they had started to receive food stamp benefits since the fall, and all said that they had not. Then, as with the early group, the interviewer provided the delayed group with the dollar amount in food stamps for which they were eligible, and then followed up to determine the proportion that went ahead and applied for food stamps. While conducting the first follow-up with the delayed group, the interviewer conducted a second follow-up with the early group.

Both groups reacted similarly to the information. Those who were eligible for more than $40 per month in either group went ahead and applied for food stamps, while generally, those who were eligible for under $40 per month tended not to apply for benefits. Findings from the first group suggest that if households did not act on the information within the first six weeks, they did not act on it at a later date.

Different Samples Design

If an evaluator is concerned about the threat of testing and if there are a large number of participants in the treatment and the control group, she should consider drawing from the treatment group and control groups pretest samples that have different individuals from the posttest samples. Considering only the treatment group, O_1 would be a sample of those who will receive the treatment. O_2 would be a different sample, and anyone who was in the first sample would be ineligible to be in the second sample. In statistical terms, this is called sampling without replacement. A similar process would be used to draw the two samples for the control group.

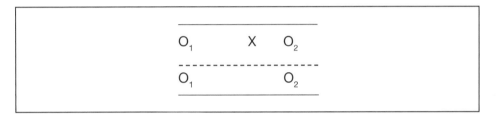

Source: Cook and Campbell (1979), p. 115.

The vertical line after the first observation represents that the samples of the first and second observations are drawn from the same population (treatment or control), but are different units.

For example, perhaps you want to learn whether an advertising blitz changes people's perceptions of a political candidate. The fear is that once people have been asked about the candidate, their perceptions of the candidate might change by the second time they are asked, simply because they became more aware of the candidate after the first observation (the threat of testing). So, rather than follow the same people over time, you would instead derive the observations from independent samples.

For the treatment group, the first observation derives from responses from a randomly chosen sample of people who will be targets of the advertising campaign. The second observation, collected after the completion of the advertising blitz, derives from a sample of people who were targets but did not provide data for the first observation. Similarly, for the control group, the first observation derives from survey responses from a population that the blitz will not target (perhaps because they do not reside in the geographic area that the blitz focused upon), and the second observation occurs after the blitz, but from a different sample of nontargeted people. By structuring observations in this way, this design addresses the threat of testing. An individual can only provide information for exactly one of the responses; no one is asked the same set of questions twice.

This design is particularly useful when simply asking the questions is likely to influence the outcome. Thus, it is particularly applicable to the arts. For example, evaluators might expect a museum exhibit to change one's thoughts on an issue. To show this, you would derive the pre-exhibit observation from a randomly drawn sample of people and a post-exhibit observation from a different sample. These samples represent the population from which they are drawn, within statistical sampling error.

If you only had these two data points, even if the exhibit visitors showed a change, the statement would be limited to "People who see the exhibit change their perspective on this issue more than those who have not seen the exhibit." This statement is quite limited because of selection issues—a select group have seen the exhibit. Those who intended to see the exhibit might have been more open to changing their perspective on the issue (selection). Further, this finding may have little generalizability because of the unique character of the treatment group. That is, although the design addresses the threat of testing, it does not address the threat of selection or the likelihood of low external validity in this example, depending on the population sampled.

When testing poses a serious threat to internal validity, this design can strengthen the evaluation research, depending on the sample size. However, this design does not address the threat of selection.

Nonequivalent Observations Drawn from One Group

A less common design used when a control group may not be possible to obtain is a design that uses the same people for the treatment group *and* the control group. The essence of this design is that it conducts measurements on only a single group of persons. The pretest measures are of two different but related constructs. The intervention is intended to affect only one of the constructs.

$$O_{1A} \quad X \quad O_{2A}$$
$$O_{1B} \qquad O_{2B}$$

Source: Cook and Campbell (1979), p. 118.

In this design, the intervention is intended to affect only the indicator of the A construct and not the indicator of the B construct. The B observation acts as the control. However, if A and B are related, because of spillover effects within the same units, it is difficult to imagine an intervention that affects only A and not B. This aspect of the design makes it quite weak. A dotted line is not needed between the treatment and control groups because the same unit acts as its own control observation.

This design might be used for a tutoring program intended to teach people one subject, but not the other. For example, consider a mathematics tutoring program. O_{1A} might be mathematics preprogram test scores and O_{1B} might represent verbal preprogram test scores. If the program is effective, one would expect an increase in the mathematics scores—but not the verbal scores. But if the tutoring program taught students studying skills while teaching them math, then the program could have substantial spillover effects.

The strength of this design comes from its use of the same people in both the treatment and control groups. Its weakness derives from the challenge of conceptualizing two observations that are closely related—but the intervention would only affect one of the measures.

Nonequivalent Groups Using Switched Measures

Related to the previous two designs is one that exploits the existence of two measures that both sufficiently measure the outcome construct. The benefit of this design is that both groups receive the treatment concurrently and that it avoids the threat of testing.

Group I O_{1A} X O_{2B}

Group II O_{1B} X O_{2A}

In this design, the total group of people who receive the treatment are divided into two subgroups (I and II). The first observation of one subgroup is the outcome measure A, and the first subgroup's second observation is of the outcome measure B. For the second group, B is the first measure and A the second.

For this design to be useful, the two subgroups must be statistically similar. If people are randomly assigned to one of the two subgroups, then this assumption by design is valid. Also, one must assume that subgroup I's pretreatment A measure is a proxy for

Group I O_{1A} X $O_{2A \text{ (drawn from Group II)}}$

$O_{2A \text{ (assuming that } O_{1A} \text{ would not have changed)}}$

Group II O_{1B} X $O_{2B \text{ (drawn from Group I)}}$

$O_{2B \text{ (assuming that } O_{1B} \text{ would not have changed)}}$

TABLE 6.1. Yad Vashem Holocaust Museum Evaluation Design.

Grand Survey	Survey I	Survey II
Demographic and background questions	Demographic and background questions	Demographic and background questions
Holocaust knowledge and views questions, set A	Holocaust knowledge and views questions, set A	
Holocaust knowledge and views questions, set B		Holocaust knowledge and views questions, set B

Source: Bickman and Hamner, 1998.

subgroup II's pretreatment A measure and similarly, subgroup II's pretreatment B measure is a proxy for subgroup II's pretreatment B measure. Another assumption is that the pretreatment measures of A and B would not have changed without the treatment. If these assumptions are valid, then the design reduces as shown in the bottom box on the facing page.

This is exactly the design used in Bickman and Hamner's study (1998) of the impact of Yad Vashem Holocaust Museum on visitors. They designed a survey with three parts (Table 6.1). One section of the survey measured a respondent's demographics and background information. The second and third sections contain a series of questions that asked sets of questions about one's knowledge and views of the Holocaust.

Those questions were divided into two parts. Part A measured knowledge and views, as did Part B. However, Part B did not contain any of the questions from Part A of the survey. From the grand survey, two different surveys were created that ostensibly measured the same construct, one's knowledge and views of the Holocaust.

Testing was a very real concern. The fear was that if respondents were asked identical questions twice, their knowledge and views about the exact issues could have changed because having seen the questions the first time would have influenced their response if asked the same questions again.

Before entering the museum, a person receives either survey I or II. The assignment of the first survey was done randomly. Upon exit from the museum, the respondent is given the other survey. Using this design, responses from both surveys from both groups are used to measure the short-term impact of the museum on visitors.

Cohort Designs

A **cohort** is defined as a group that experienced the same event at the same time. One example is birth cohorts, whose members were all born within the same time period (such as within a given year). Alternatively, a cohort could be a group of people who enter a graduate program at the same time. These people are likely to have been born in different years, and perhaps in different decades, yet they all experienced the beginning of their graduate education simultaneously. The concept of cohorts also applies to programs, where a cohort can be a group of people who go through a program at the same time.

The concept of a cohort can be used for evaluation purposes. It is often reasonable to assume that a cohort differs only in minor ways from cohorts that immediately precede or follow the cohort. Take a group of children who enter second grade in a school district in 2006. It is likely that they will differ in minor ways, if at all, from children in the district who entered second grade in 2005 and 2007.

When a treatment is provided to one cohort, assuming that contiguous cohorts would otherwise appear similar, the treatment's effects can be inferred by examining the differences in outcomes between the contiguous cohorts. For example, if in 2006 the second graders were introduced to a new mathematics curriculum, assuming that proficiency in math would have otherwise been similar between the 2005 and 2006 cohorts, any differences that appear would be inferred to have been caused by the new curriculum.

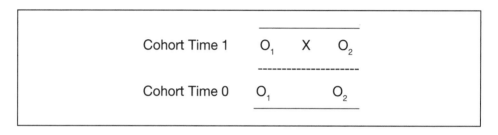

Applying the design to this example, math proficiency of children entering second grade in 2006 is compared with math proficiency of children entering second grade in 2005. The second grade observation must occur before receiving the new curriculum. Third grade scores are used as the "posttest."

If the second grade observation does not occur before receiving the new curriculum, then one would want to add on another pretest observation, which could be the first grade scores. Considering the first grade score would also strengthen the design because it would show that the two cohorts had similar patterns of growth before the treatment (change in curriculum). Further, adding on another posttest observation would reveal whether the change in test scores is long-lasting, or whether there is a lagged effect.

$$O_{\text{1st grade (2005)}} \quad O_{\text{2nd grade (2006)}} \quad X \quad O_{\text{3rd grade (2007)}} \quad O_{\text{4th grade (2008)}}$$

$$O_{\text{1st grade (2004)}} \quad O_{\text{2nd grade (2005)}} \quad O_{\text{3rd grade (2006)}} \quad O_{\text{4th grade (2007)}}$$

Cohort designs tend to rely on archival data. The designs are most useful when there is a clear point at which the cohorts were provided with different treatments. The design has obvious applications to school settings, where there is a steady stream of cohorts. However, the design can be applied in any number of settings, for example, to human resource practices in companies, where the cohorts are defined as a group of employees who start with a company within a given period, and the treatment could be changes in orientation procedures. It can also naturally be applied to age groups, in terms of a treatment or intervention that occurred that affected people according to their age.

The key feature of the design is that the observations for the cohorts actually occur at different time periods. The evaluator must keep clear when the intervention occurred and whether the contiguous cohorts are actually comparable groups. If done correctly, quasi-experimental designs that rely on cohort differences can be quite powerful. But the threat of history could be serious if events occurred outside of the program that would have affected the assumption of comparability between the cohorts.

Time Series Designs

Time series follow the same "unit"—people, households, neighborhoods, and so on—over time. Such data are called longitudinal data. The key feature of longitudinal data is that the same unit is followed over consecutive periods. In the simplest pretest and posttest design with a control group, the units of analysis are followed for two time periods, and in the delayed treatment design, they are followed for three. In time series designs, the same units are followed for multiple time periods, both before and after the treatment. We start with the simplest, which does not have a control group.

$$O_1 \quad O_2 \quad O_3 \quad O_4 \quad O_5 \quad X \quad O_6 \quad O_7 \quad O_8 \quad O_9 \quad O_{10}$$

Source: Cook and Campbell (1979), p. 209.

This design does not have a control group because the pretreatment measures should be enough to establish a pattern that would suggest that in the absence of the treatment the pattern would have continued. The design is illustrated arbitrarily with sixteen observations. There is no fixed number on the number of observations needed to establish a time series. The number of observations should be large enough to establish a pattern both before and after the treatment.

A change in the slope, intercept, or functional form of the pattern would suggest that the treatment was effective. The threat of history curtails the evaluator's ability to draw causal conclusions from the data. You would want to consider whether other concurrent treatments could have produced the effect rather than the treatment, or could have contributed to at least a portion of the change. Further, there could have been countervailing forces that would have upset the pretreatment pattern even if the treatment had not occurred.

If a treatment has immediate effects, then you can limit the examination of the threat of history to the time period immediately surrounding the treatment. However, if the treatment has lagged effects, then one would need to consider any other events that could have affected the observations for an even greater length of time.

The treatment could change the slope, intercept, or pretreatment pattern that was established. It is important to be aware of patterns of seasonality; some outcomes are seasonal, and treatments could change the seasonal pattern.

Imagine a program designed to provide seasonal construction workers with employment opportunities during the winter months. Such a program is intended to disrupt the seasonal pattern. A summer reading program is intended to decrease "summer back-slide" among schoolchildren. The program has years of data showing that children's reading abilities increase during the school year but after summer break, their reading abilities were below what they were in the previous June. The program is intended to change this pattern of summer backslide. In this case, there is no reason to expect a lag in the program's effects and there is probably no need for a control group. A control group would strengthen the causal argument, but the pretreatment time series may be sufficient to convince most who consider the program's effects.

The time series with a control group allows evaluators to better consider whether the threat of history has impacted the posttreatment level and pattern of the outcome(s).

Naturally, in this design if the treatment has an effect, one would expect to see the effect only in the treatment group.

$$O_1 \quad O_2 \quad O_3 \quad O_4 \quad O_5 \; X \; O_6 \quad O_7 \quad O_8 \quad O_9 \quad O_{10}$$

$$O_1 \quad O_2 \quad O_3 \quad O_4 \quad O_5 \quad O_6 \quad O_7 \quad O_8 \quad O_9 \quad O_{10}$$

Source: Cook and Campbell (1979), p. 214.

Another time-series pattern to consider is the treatment–removed treatment pattern. Here, the treatment is applied and then later removed, with the expectation that after the treatment's application, an effect would exist, and when the treatment was removed, the effect would cease. Although some treatments may have such a mechanical cause-and-effect relationship, many treatments do not. Some treatments have long-lasting effects, and their effects can continue beyond the application of the treatment. That is, some causes produce irreversible effects.

$$O_1 \ O_2 \ O_3 \ X \ O_4 \ O_5 \ O_6 \ \overline{X} \ O_7 \ O_8 \ O_9 \ X \ O_{10} \ O_{11} \ O_{12} \ \overline{X} \ O_{13} \ O_{14} \ X \ O_{15} \ O_{16}$$

Further, it may be impossible to "remove" many types of treatments. For example, treatments that relay information cannot be "removed" (unless the memories of participants are erased, which of course would not pass the muster of an institutional review board!).

The removed treatment design is most useful in the policy arena, where public policies may be implemented for finite time spans, and then stopped. Or, alternate public policies could exist over time. If the design is applied without a control group, then the application of the treatments may interact with the threat of history. Even if there is a control group, you would have to be concerned about history and perhaps the threat of selection.

Examples of this design in the public policy arena include David and Wright's famous paper (1971) on abortion policy in Romania in the 1960s. They found that when abortion was allowed, the health of infants was better than when abortion was not permitted. You could possibly use this design to examine the effects of tax cuts to the wealthy under President George W. Bush, which were designed to "sunset"—that is, if the cuts actually do cease in the future.

Archival Data

Time series designs often depend on archival or historical data. You should be careful when using archival data for two reasons—the threat of mono-operation bias and the threat of instrumentation.

The threat of mono-operation bias appears because typically there will be only one way that the treatment and effect were historically operationalized. An evaluator is often constrained by having to work with the data and operationalizations that have been used over the time period, even if they are not perfect or even good measures of the constructs of interest. Thus, the evaluation research becomes quite constrained by what data have been collected in the past. The questions that the current evaluation activities are investigating may not even have been issues in the past, and the data collected may not be a very good fit with the current evaluation questions.

When using historical data, you must be acutely aware of whether the data collection systems or the definitions of the indicators changed over time. There could have been subtle changes that affected the level or pattern of an indicator. For example, if you were examining a time series of racial statistics in the United States, you would have to be acutely aware that in the 2000 census, respondents were allowed to report more than one racial category. This change has had ramifications on all government statistics reported by race. For example, in 2003, labor force statistics for African Americans excluded anyone who reported that they were both African American and at least one other race. That is, if someone reported themselves as black and white, then they were excluded from post-2003 labor force statistics for African Americans and also from statistics for the white population.

The threat of instrumentation derives not only from the possibility of changed definitions over time, but also from changes in the data collection processes that may have occurred. For example, if relying on survey data, you must inquire exactly how the data were collected over the period of the data being used. If at one time data collection relied on a mail-back survey design, and then the data collection transitioned to a telephone survey design, the change in the collection approach could have ramifications on the quality of the data and the achieved sample.

Changes in the sampling frame, response rates, and the achieved sample may also have ramifications on the measures. For these reasons, you should carefully examine and have an understanding of archival data before relying on it for evaluation purposes. Archival data are inflexible. If appropriate, the data can reveal insights into the long-term effects of treatments. However, you should be cautious about using such data when indicators do not closely align with the constructs of interest, or when changes have occurred in the definitions or data collection systems.

SUMMARY

The challenge presented to evaluators is to choose the quasi-experimental design that is most appropriate for a given situation. This involves considering the data collection opportunities that exist as well as ethical limitations. This chapter presents most of Cook and Campbell's classical quasi-experimental designs, which are actually used in evaluation research, but the evaluator may create a new design, mixing favorable elements of the above designs.

KEY TERMS

archival data

cohort

delayed treatment control group design

different samples design

longitudinal data

one-group posttest-only design

one-group pretest-posttest design

posttest-only design with nonequivalent groups

quasi-experimental design

quasi-experimental notation

nonequivalent groups using switched measures
nonequivalent observations design drawn
  from one group

time series
untreated control group design
  with pretest and posttest

DISCUSSION QUESTIONS

1. Explain how a clear understanding of the threats to validity impact the quasi-experimental design chosen to evaluate a program.

2. What are the benefits and concerns with using control groups?

3. The program you are evaluating has a wealth of archival data collected under three different program leaders over a twelve-year period. What concerns do you have about the usefulness of this data to your evaluation?

CHAPTER

7

COLLECTING DATA

LEARNING OBJECTIVES

After reading this chapter, you should be able to

- Select an appropriate approach for collecting data
- Initiate a protocol whose data will fit the chosen design

An evaluator can take a variety of approaches to collecting relevant data. This chapter outlines various approaches, starting with informal interviews and finishing with survey design. Regardless of the approach used to collect data, an evaluator should proceed with a well-thought-out protocol, which will ultimately result in data that can be used in the chosen quasi-experimental design.

INFORMAL INTERVIEWS

As discussed in Chapter Two, informal interviews with stakeholders must be done initially to develop an understanding of the program. The interviews are more or less conversations, and though they can provide useful insights into the subject matter, they cannot lead to statements regarding the frequency of issues.

Beyond helping to develop an understanding of the program, informal interviews can be used to understand issues surrounding the need for the program and its possible success. They can also highlight the stories of individual cases, and as such, they are commonly known as anecdotes. Anecdotal information can be useful to develop an awareness of possible issues, but does not substitute for formal, purposeful data collection.

FOCUS GROUPS

Focus groups are similar to informal interviews in that they provide insights but cannot reveal the propensity of an occurrence in the population. A focus group consists of people who are willing to share their thoughts, attitudes, and experiences. Think of a focus group as a dinner party with a leader-evaluator who uses open-ended questions, when needed, to stimulate conversation. A focus group differs from an informal survey in that in the latter, the interaction is limited to that between the interviewer and respondent. In a focus group, the group dynamics can lead to a topic of conversation that is totally unanticipated by the leader-evaluator. Personal experience shows that focus groups are more likely to provide insights into unanticipated issues than are informal interviews. One person's perspective can trigger another person to respond with a related, unexpected perspective or experience, thus opening up a new avenue of inquiry.

Focus groups can be a way to discover areas of inquiry that you would like to include in a formal survey, and in that sense be a means to the end of designing a thorough survey. In this sense, the focus groups should be conducted before the start of survey data collection.

Alternatively, one may decide to collect data only through focus groups. Used in this way, the focus groups are not a means to designing a survey but an end in and of themselves. For example, you might conduct focus groups to find out the issues that concern the program's population. Focus groups could help identify different experiences that clients have had with the program. If you were interested in the perspective of service providers, then you could conduct focus groups with only the providers to better understand the system and the issues with which providers are concerned.

After becoming aware of the existence of issues, if you wanted to know the **propensity of issues**, then you would include the areas of inquiry you learned about through the informal interviews and focus groups on a **formal survey instrument**.

Evaluators have different styles in conducting focus groups, and a review of sociology and marketing methodology texts will reveal a variety of approaches. The style advocated below evolved from experiences in conducting focus groups with a variety of types of stakeholders.

The size of the group should be limited to between five and nine people, with a strong preference for six to eight—the size of an intimate dinner party.

Plan to conduct a number of focus groups; exactly how many, though, cannot be determined a priori. Theoretically, collecting information via focus groups should continue until no new issues or perspectives are revealed. That is, continue until subsequent groups do not reveal new information. For simple issues with a homogeneous client population, the number of groups conducted could be as low as two or three, but for more complex issues where a variety of perspectives are needed, you might run a dozen different focus groups.

With respect to the length of the focus group session, ninety minutes is usually appropriate. Exceeding ninety minutes would make participants tired and could jeopardize the quality of the information being collected. It usually takes approximately thirty minutes at the beginning of the session for people in the group to feel comfortable with each other and the setting. Allow time at the end of the session, perhaps about ten to fifteen minutes, for participants to make last-minute observations. In a ninety-minute session, that leaves only forty-five minutes for high-quality interaction.

In some cases, it may be necessary to very carefully compose the groups. You might want to limit the group to similarly situated people. For example, when interviewing staff, you might want to assure that different people at different levels of the organization are not in the same group. If the topic has different effects on subpopulations, then you might want to stratify the groups by subpopulations. For example, when genders are affected in different ways, or have varying perspectives, you might want to have a group of men and one of women.

Another way of composing groups is to consider the process involved. The composition of the group would depend on how people are affected by or participate in a process, possibly resulting in a group including different people at various levels of an organization, or a mixture of very different types of clients. It is important to carefully consider what is wanted out of the group and how its composition could promote or impede that goal. Sometimes, a random sampling of the population might suffice if you want different perspectives to have the opportunity of participating in the group.

Once you have decided the parameters of the group's composition, then you need to decide exactly how people will be able to become a part of the group. There are three distinct approaches: (1) passively asking for people to participate in a group, (2) actively asking for volunteers, and (3) purposely recruiting particular types of participants.

In the first approach (passive recruitment, with a sign or ad containing the leader's contact information), unless the level of compensation for participating in the group is high enough that everybody would want to be a part of the group, it is likely that those who volunteer for the group differ from those who do not volunteer. Volunteers may differ with respect to their experience with the issue or program, and may be more likely to have had either an exceptionally good or bad experience with the program. If the focus group aims to learn about the possible range of experiences with the program, then this approach may suffice. Thus, to decrease selection bias, you should offer compensation sufficient enough to overcome a potential participant's reluctance to participate. Exactly what the level of compensation might be depends on the target population. The compensation should be large enough so that most people will agree to participate in the group. In one study, low-income participants were given twenty-dollar coupons to a local grocery store, and this level seemed to induce cooperation. However, that level of compensation may not be great enough to induce participation of a higher-income population.

It is not uncommon for studies to offer child care to parents while they are participating in a focus group, thinking that such an offer will reduce barriers to parents' participation. Such an offer may appear to reduce a barrier, but in practice many parents are not comfortable leaving their children in an unfamiliar situation; thus, the barrier would remain. The barrier could be more effectively reduced if parents were provided money to compensate for child-care costs they may have incurred. The researcher should think through any potential barriers to participation and establish procedures that will effectively reduce barriers.

Evaluators differ on whether compensation should be provided. In practice, without compensating participants, an aberrant sample is likely to result—only those abnormally interested in the issue will respond, and ultimately evaluators will not be able to generalize findings because the sample does not represent any known population. To attract both those who are moderately interested and those who are abnormally interested in the subject of the focus group, you must compensate participants for their time. The same strategy pertains to the target population of surveys.

There are alternative approaches toward recruiting focus group participants, ranging on a continuum of passive recruitment to active recruitment. In passive recruitment efforts, such as flyers that advertise the study or using mass media to recruit volunteers, the onus is on the potential participant to decide to join the study and figure out how to enroll. Instead, an active recruitment approach targets particular individuals for participation and attempts to help them overcome barriers to participation—for example, by sending a letter to everybody in a neighborhood informing them of the need for participants and following up on the letter with a telephone call. Active approaches are superior because they make it easier for participants to join, thus resulting in a more appropriate sample.

Some researchers advocate the use of electronic equipment to record a focus group. This approach certainly allows the researchers to review the exact content of the group. However, participants may not feel free to discuss a topic if they believe that they are being recorded making statements. If you envision that sensitive issues could arise during the course of the session, then you should investigate alternative approaches to recording the content of the group.

An approach that works well for sensitive topics is to run the session with a research team consisting of a group leader-facilitator and an assistant. The leader interacts with the participants, and the assistant's role is limited to taking detailed handwritten notes. When the leader explains to participants that they will only be identified by a number and a general description (usually limited to gender, age, and perhaps race) participants generally feel more at ease with the handwritten approach. The increase in their comfort level allows participants to speak freely and ultimately yields higher-quality information.

Rather than conduct the group face-to-face at a physical setting, another approach is to ask participants to be part of a conference call. This approach has advantages and disadvantages. The cost and convenience of being a part of a conference call makes this option attractive. However, the face-to-face interaction is sacrificed, which in some circumstances could be beneficial but in others detrimental. Evaluators should think through whether this option is appropriate for the focus group's subject matter.

Regardless of the exact approach used, the leader should prepare for the focus group by creating a list of open-ended questions that should stimulate conversation. Closed-ended, yes or no questions, or those that have predetermined categories of responses, tend not to stimulate conversations. The leader should be aware of the possibility of not getting through all of the questions The conversation may lead to an unanticipated area or participants may delve into an issue in more depth than was anticipated.

The leader should be careful about intervening in the conversation and should intervene only when the conversation goes astray for a long period, lags, or is dominated by one or more participants to the extent that others cannot participate. It is natural for conversation to go astray for short periods of time—in fact, that is often the purpose of running the session. However, if the conversation seems to be leading to a direction that is not the topic of the focus group, then the leader is obliged to intervene to bring the conversation back to the topic at hand.

Sometimes, one participant can dominate the conversation. The leader's obligation is to assure that the group's environment is such that all participants feel that their participation is valuable. The leader should take care to elicit input from all. This can be delicate, though, because some people are naturally quieter than others, and the leader certainly does not want to alienate or draw too much attention to these participants. Some participants may in fact be quiet because they are reflecting on their own experiences and views and will speak up when they feel it is appropriate.

To keep the identity of participants anonymous, in the notes participants should be referred to by their description (such as demographics, shirt color, and so on) and a number. Usually, retaining the names of participants is not necessary.

Immediately after each focus group ends, the assistant and leader should review the notes, filling in where necessary from their recollections. A draft of the report on the group should be written the same day, if possible. In this day of electronic recording, some may be skeptical of going back to this "old school" way of taking handwritten notes on the focus group's conversation. However, I have found that the increased recording capacity offered by electronically recording the groups does not outweigh its inhibiting impact.

If the groups are being used to design a survey, notes from each session should be reviewed to determine whether any new issues or new responses have emerged. If new issues surface, then the survey designer needs to determine whether the issue is significant enough to be included on the survey. Likewise, if there are new responses to issues that were already included, then the survey designer needs to determine whether the propensity of that response will be large, or whether the response is important enough to be included on the survey instrument.

To give an example, in the early 1990s, the Food Distribution Research Project in Pittsburgh was contracted to design a survey on the use of the private food assistance network in the United States. It was the first large survey on this topic. Focus groups were used to discover the issues and possible responses to questions for inclusion on the survey. A number of focus groups had already been conducted where participants were asked why they started using the private food assistance network (that is, food pantries and food banks). In one of the final focus groups, one woman spoke up and said that medical bills were the catalyst for her relying on a food pantry. Her tragic story was that she had given birth to a baby while uninsured. The baby was not healthy, and died after a few months. The medical bills faced by the parents drove them to relying on a food pantry for groceries.

In the early 1990s, the health insurance crisis had not reached most people's consciousness to the extent that it has today. Surely, the response of "medical bills" or "medical debts" would not have been included on the survey had that woman not revealed her experience. Although the research team was uncertain of how many others might have been driven to rely on a food pantry for this reason, the response seemed important enough in a policy context to include on the survey. The survey results consequently showed a substantial number who were driven to use a food pantry because of medical bills.

SURVEY DESIGN

Surveys are used when evaluators know the issues to inquire about and have a good idea of the possible universe of responses. A well-designed survey consists of the shortest set of valid and reliable questions that are placed in a way that maximizes the rate of response. Question placement on a survey should result in a survey instrument that flows like a conversation.

Question validity refers to the extent that a given response reflects what a survey designer intends and expects the response to mean. **Question reliability** refers to the extent to which people in comparable situations will respond to questions in similar ways. Reliability also refers to the extent that the same respondent in unchanged circumstances will respond to the same questions in the same way. With a highly reliable survey, if a respondent was surveyed at two points in time and the respondent's circumstances or views had not changed, the respondent would provide identical responses at the two points in time. Measurement error derives from the extent that a question is unreliable and potentially not valid.

Surveys differ from unstructured interviews and focus groups. *Surveys are used to discover the frequency of issues and views, whereas informal interviews and focus groups are used to discover the issues that exist and the range of circumstances and views.* In informal interviews, all of the questions should be open-ended questions (such as "Could you please describe today's weather?"). However, in surveys, nearly all questions should be presented in a closed-ended format. For example, one could ask the following question on a survey:

Please place a "Y" if the description of the weather applies to today's weather conditions, and an "N" if it does not apply to today's weather:

_____

_____ Sunny

_____ Cloudy

_____ Some chance of rain

_____ Raining

_____ Snowing

_____ Hailing

_____ Other (please describe):

_____

Not only must questions be asked identically of all respondents, but respondents must bear the same burden of providing a response. In open-ended questions, respondents bear the burden of providing an appropriate response. Responses between respondents can vary because of differences in their willingness or ability to articulate or provide a response.

An open-ended question about the weather could be: "Please describe today's weather." In this case, the respondent needs to think of all of the ways that one could describe the weather. Respondents could provide different responses not only because they perceive the weather differently, but also because they use different terminology to describe the weather or have not considered the degree of humidity, precipitation, and sunshine all as part of the weather. If respondents take on a different burden to answer the question (for example, some respondents may spend more time than others pondering the question, or some respondents may provide a more complete response to the question), then responses may differ because of varying perceptions of how to form a complete and proper response.

Another reason to avoid open-ended questions on a survey is that analyzing such questions is extremely burdensome for the evaluators. First, the responses from the open-ended questions must be entered into a database exactly as the respondents gave them. Unless you are planning to report all responses, categories of responses should be created and each response should be placed into a category. Determining appropriate categories by which to organize the data and fitting each open-ended response into a category post-survey requires thought and manpower. It is far more efficient to have thought through the appropriate categories of responses and included them on the survey from the beginning, instead of having to go back and retrofit open-ended responses.

The only reason for an open-ended question to be on a survey is so that respondents feel that their unique voices have been heard. Open-ended questions on surveys often indicate that the survey designer did not do his or her homework beforehand.

Information gleaned from focus groups and informal interviews helps to design closed-ended questions, as these sessions will reveal the bulk of possible responses to questions. Thus, if the survey designer knows that the survey will include an issue but does not know what the possible responses may be, the focus groups should bear out that information. It is wise, though, to leave a category for closed-ended questions—such as "other, please explain"—providing space for respondents to give a response that was not included on the survey.

Before designing a survey, you should become familiar with how others have inquired about similar issues for two reasons. First, others may have asked the questions in a good way, and if the questions are not copyrighted, they could be included on your survey instrument. Second, you may ultimately want to compare results from your survey with results that others have obtained on the same or different populations. To accomplish this easily, the questions must be asked and responses constructed in exactly the same way.

Because evaluators might analyze responses by demographic characteristics, it is usually important for a survey to collect demographic information. Certainly, if conducting a survey in the United States, you would want to become familiar with how the U.S. Census Bureau asks demographic questions on its most recent census (see www.census.gov). Appendix A includes the U.S. Census Bureau's 2000 Short Form and the Long Form. The Long Form is the basis for local level economic and social data. Even if evaluators disagree with how the U.S. Census Bureau has asked demographic questions, they will probably want to be able to compare the demographics of their survey population with the U.S. population, or a subpopulation of the United States. If evaluators decide to ask demographic questions differently from the U.S. Census Bureau's practices, then they forfeit the opportunity to make such direct comparisons. For example, if a program serves the population in a municipality, you would probably want to comment on how the program's population compares with the municipality's population, as reflected in the most current census, in many relevant demographic dimensions. If evaluators do not ask for demographic characteristics in the same way they were asked in the most recent census, then they will not be able to make such a comparison. As the government's questions are not copyrighted, you can simply borrow the questions as they appear on the census.

The same principle applies when comparing results from a survey with results from other surveys on the topic. If other programs to which the program at hand would like to compare itself have collected data and asked questions in a specific way, evaluators must ask their questions in the same way in order to do a direct comparison. For example, if a program has asked about the hunger status of its clients and wants to compare these responses with those of food pantry clients as measured in America's Second Harvest's 2006 Hunger in America survey, then the program should ask questions exactly as worded on the previous survey.

Before creating new questions, evaluators should be aware of how questions measuring the same construct have been worded in other surveys. The survey designer must do his or her homework on this step, which could take a considerable amount of time. The designer should review the literature on the topic to discover which surveys have already been done and then obtain the actual survey instruments used. Not only does the designer want to use the same question, but she should be cognizant of where the questions were placed within other surveys, because the placement and context of the question could skew question responses. A designer may run up against proprietary problems, where previous questions have been copyrighted and cannot be used without permission.

Survey designers differ in their opinions of where demographic questions should appear on a survey. A fairly recent trend has been to place such questions at the end, the rationale being that these questions tend to be alienating and are not the heart of the survey.

Others prefer placing the questions at the very beginning of the survey, for two reasons. First, if people are reluctant to provide such basic information, they may be reluctant to provide topical information, and second, if respondents do not complete the survey, one would want to know how their demographics differ from those who complete the entire survey.

The following are general but simple rules in survey design:

■ **Keep the survey as short as possible.** Each question added decreases the probability that the respondent will complete the survey or that he will agree to being surveyed at all. There is a trade-off between short surveys that provide a snapshot of an issue, and longer ones that may delve into one issue's interaction with another. Evaluators want quality data that yield insight into a problem, but they should carefully consider the burden on respondents when adding each and every question.

■ **Avoid "yes bias."** Research shows that respondents prefer to answer "yes" more than "no"—people like to agree. Word the questions in a way that would prevent this bias. For example, rather than ask "Do you like the weather today?" use the question "What do you like about the weather today?" with various categories of responses, including "nothing" (which would substitute for a "no" response).

- **Vary the format of questions throughout the survey.** The goal is to get the respondent to think about the response that he provides. Faced with a long list of questions asked in the same way, the respondent may be tempted to go down the list and provide the same response, without thinking through each question. This is especially common in written surveys, but it does occur in surveys administered by an interviewer. Often, this happens when people are asked to "rate" a series of items, perhaps how much the respondents like something. Just as respondents wouldn't want to have a conversation that was monotonous, the survey instrument should not be monotonous, or it will yield poor-quality data.

- **Make the "look" of the survey user-friendly.** Use large type, spacing, and even color to make the survey easy for the respondent to understand and complete. Small type discourages completion of the survey, especially for the elderly and people who require reading glasses (the majority of the population over forty years of age!).

Once you have designed a survey that on paper seems as good as possible, it must be pretested to assure that it is collecting the information that you intend it to collect, that it flows appropriately, and does not seem confusing.

There are many ways to pretest a survey instrument. Psychological pretesting has the respondent talk through, while taking the survey, how she is thinking about the questions. This approach is not commonly used because it is expensive and time-consuming.

A more usual approach is to administer the survey to individuals under conditions similar to those in which the survey will ultimately be administered, and then informally interview the respondents immediately after they complete the survey. If the survey is written or Web-based, the designer might want to be present so that the respondent can ask any questions right then and there. Afterwards, the designer will ask the respondent questions about how she completed the survey to make sure that the data collected were what the designer intended.

After the first few pretests, the designer will revise the survey instrument accordingly. The second and all subsequent drafts will then need to be pretested. Pretesting and revising should continue until all kinks are addressed.

Sometimes, if the survey is revised substantially or if a significant amount of time has passed between the pretest and the time that all other respondents complete their surveys, the data collected from respondents in the pre-test cannot be used in the final data set. However, sometimes they may be usable data, the evaluator should use her judgment to decide this.

SAMPLING

The other aspect of collecting data by survey is to decide who will be asked to complete the survey and how data will be collected. You may be able to run focus groups and design a good survey, but you should also consult with a local statistician about the particular sampling opportunities and challenges of the data collection scheme.

This section provides only a very broad overview of various sampling approaches. I hope that this section will show that there may not be a need to survey every program participant and, in fact, that it may be undesirable to do so. You may be able to acquire information of acceptable quality without going to the expense of surveying an entire population. A statistician at a local university or college may be able to assist in the design of the sample, perhaps for a fee—but this fee is likely to be small in comparison with the amount of work that can be saved in reducing data collection down to the smallest and most manageable undertaking.

A **census** is a situation where the data collector intends to collect information from 100 percent of the units in the universe, but this is not always appropriate or necessary. A **sample** collects information from less than 100 percent of the units in the universe. Collecting information from less than 100 percent of the population may suffice if you believe that an estimate of the true population value is acceptable for your purposes. For example, rather than asking all program participants about their experience with a program, you may be able to use the data from a sample of the participants to approximate the experience of all participants. The extent to which the sample estimate varies from the population estimate is known as the **sampling error**.

There are many ways of achieving a sample of the population. The critical aspect of a formal sample is that all in the universe must have some probability of having been selected into the sample.

A **convenience sample**, which is created at the convenience of the data collectors, does not meet the above criterion and is not a formal sampling approach. An example is a situation where a data collector was interested in the degree to which a population's human rights were being violated, or the per capita rate of human rights violations. To collect the data, a human rights worker set up a location where people who had suffered human rights abuses could report such abuses. Naturally, only people who know about the data collection and who suffered human rights abuses would report the abuses. The data that results from this type of system will not allow evaluators to estimate the rate of human rights abuses, per one thousand people, in the population. The data do not yield an estimate because people were not purposefully sampled.

Similarly, a **"snowball" sample** is not a purposeful sample. Snowball samples occur when, after one case with the characteristic is discovered, the data collector asks the person reporting the incident for references to other similar cases. In the human rights example, a snowball sample would be created when the first person who experienced human rights abuses refers data collectors to another victim, who would become the next case in the sample. The sample grows because of referrals from people already in the sample, hence the term "snowball."

A snowball sample cannot yield population estimates of the incidence of an event, because evaluators do not know the degree to which people who were not included in the sample experienced the event. A per capita rate of the occurrence of an event in a population is calculated by dividing the total number of times the event occurred by the number of people in the population. Even if some people who were entered into the snowball sample did not have their human rights abused, it is likely that the sample that results does not represent the population as a whole. Everybody in the population did not have a known probability of being included in the survey sample.

Another approach is to create what is known as a **simple random sample.** The key to developing this kind of sample is that there must be a list from which to draw sampled units. That is, starting with a list of every unit in the universe, evaluators decide upon the sample size. The sample size that is needed is a function of the population size and the estimate's degree of acceptable error. Every unit on the list has the same chance of being entered into the sample. By chance (or using a random number generator found in most spreadsheet packages), units are selected to be in the sample.

Consider a situation where evaluators want to know the proportion of people in a town who had their human rights violated at the hands of the police in a given year. The town has fifty thousand people in it. If you conducted a census on the issue, each and every person in the town would need to be asked whether they experienced a human rights violation in the past year. This approach would be not only expensive but very time consuming. Instead, you could apply simple random sampling to the population. An estimate that was within (plus or minus) 4 percent of the estimate's true value in the population would suffice in this example. If one suspects that each individual has a 50 percent chance of having had her human rights violated, then one would need to interview approximately six hundred randomly selected people.

The mathematical relationship between sample size and the variance of the estimate from the true population value is

$$1.96 * \sqrt{(p(1 - p)/n)} = \text{Margin of error}$$

Solving this equation assuming a 50 percent chance of a violation having occurred (which is the worst case scenario that would yield the largest sample size) and that a 4 percent margin of error is acceptable, one gets

$$1.96 * \sqrt{((.5 * .5)/n)} = .04$$

and the needed sample size, n, is 600.

If you believe that that the chance of a violation having occurred is only 20 percent, then the formula reduces to

$$1.96 * \sqrt{((.2 * .8)/n)} = .04$$

and the needed sample size becomes 384.

Another approach to sampling is a stratified random sample. A simple random sample, as shown above, allows each unit in the universe to have the same probability of being selected. However, there are times when the evaluator may want to design a sample that guarantees that enough minority units in the universe get into the sample, so that statistics can be calculated for the minority as well as the majority units. For example, an evaluator may believe that there is a difference in the propensity of human rights violations depending on ethnicity. If someone from group A (a minority group) was arrested, it is more likely that he would suffer abuse in prison than someone from group B. If a simple random sample approach was used in this case, there may not be enough people from Group A for the evaluator to compare the experiences of arrestees from Group A and Group B. To assure that both groups have a large enough sample, evaluators essentially divide the population in two on the basis of ethnicity, which gives those in Group A a higher chance of being included in the sample than those in Group B. The evaluator has stratified, or separated, the sample and assigned different probabilities of being selected, depending on ethnicity.

Other times when evaluators may want to use stratified random sampling include when a program is offered at many sites. The evaluator would want to assure that a large enough sample is achieved from each of the sites in order to compare outcomes from each site. When using a stratified random sampling approach, evaluators should consult with a statistician on the drawing of the sample, the weighing of the data, and how to calculate population statistics on the basis of the sample.

WAYS TO COLLECT SURVEY DATA

In addition to having a clear idea of the survey's purpose, how the questions will appear on it, and the ideal sampling framework, evaluators also need to determine exactly how the data will be collected. The two broad approaches to collecting survey data are interviewer-administered and self-administered.

Surveys administered by an interviewer can be conducted in person in a face-to-face interview or over the telephone. Both approaches present challenges. The face-to-face survey obviously requires that the interviewer be present to talk with the respondent. If there is a captive audience, say, while potential respondents are at the program or program site, this may be possible. But if the audience is not "captive," actually making arrangements for the interviewer to meet with respondents can be expensive and challenging. One approach is for interviewers to meet respondents at a site or at their home, but this means that travel expenses may be incurred. Also, meeting respondents may introduce safety risks. Even if appointments are made, respondents sometimes do not keep the appointment (and emergencies may prevent interviewers from keeping the appointment), thus adding to the expense of collecting data in this way. Unless the benefit of collecting the information face-to-face outweighs the additional expense of doing so, you should not use this mode of data collection.

A less expensive way of collecting data is by telephone, with an interviewer reading questions to the respondent. This mode also presents challenges, not the least of which is reaching the desired sample by telephone. If surveying only program participants, it is likely that the program will have current telephone numbers for most participants.

However, telephones become disconnected and people change telephone numbers. If using the telephone to survey a general population, it may be difficult to find appropriate people to survey. One solution is to use random digit dialing, so that people with cell phones or unlisted numbers are assured of entering into the sample. When a person is reached, she must be screened to assure that she is appropriate for the survey—potentially, many numbers may need to be dialed to reach appropriate people. In random digit dialing, erroneous contacts may be made, such as businesses, disconnected telephones, or inoperative telephones, which would increase the expense of the data collection.

When an appropriate person is reached, then most surveyors use a CATI system—Computer Assisted Telephone Interview. Using CATI, an interviewer reads questions from a computer screen and enters responses directly into the computer, thus creating a database of responses. One advantage of the CATI system is that if the survey has skip patterns, where questions may be skipped depending on the responses to previous questions, the next question automatically appears on the interviewer's screen, thus reducing interviewer error. Another advantage is that the database is automatically being created, so a current database always exists. If programmed correctly, the interviewer can enter only valid responses to questions, which reduces the amount of time that an analyst might spend "cleaning" the data (that is, assuring that responses are theoretically appropriate).

Computer-based technology also allows for other modes of data collection. Web-based surveys allow for respondents to complete the survey on-line and automatically have their information included in a database. With web-based surveys, there is a temptation to not sample purposely and instead invite many to complete the survey but not keep strict track of who did and who did not start or complete the survey. This can be overcome by carefully constructing the desired sample and following up with potential respondents, as one would do with a telephone or a mail-based survey.

Mailed surveys present another mode. Again, they are expensive and give the respondent the burden of completing it on his or her own time, and thus they can yield low response rates. To address this problem, considerable tracking and follow-up may be needed. Because mail surveys are done on paper, the survey data need to be input. The survey can be designed so that it can later be scanned by a system that essentially reads respondents' answers and enters them into an electronic data set. If the sample size is large, investing in such a system may be wise.

ANONYMITY AND CONFIDENTIALITY

Survey designers often like to promise respondents that their responses to the survey will be kept "anonymous" and "confidential." Anonymity means that exactly who participated in a survey is unknown. The survey's target population is known, but the evaluator will not know who in that target population actually provided responses. Usually, responses do not become truly anonymous until after all follow-up of units is complete. The survey director needs to know who in the sample has or has not completed the survey in order to follow up only with those who have not completed the survey. To promise anonymity, after the data collection phase is over, the managers remove the names and exact street addresses and any other information that would directly identify a respondent. Rather than refer to cases as names, cases are given an identification number, which has no meaning other than being the case number for the purpose of the study. Of course, the ID number cannot be a social security number, passport number, or any other sort of number that could identify an individual. After the link between the identification of respondents and their responses is removed, if anonymity was promised there is no way to go back and determine the identification of those who participated in the survey.

Confidentiality means that the data will be held in confidence and used appropriately. Responses will never be presented at a level of detail that would allow anyone to identify the respondent. In practice, to accomplish confidentiality, in addition to not being able to release individual-level data, the evaluator cannot release information at such a small level that would allow an inquisitive person to figure out who was likely to have provided the response. For example, evaluators may not be able to present data comparing statistics in a local area on a small number of minority children with majority children, because an inquisitive reader may be able to deduce exactly to whom the statistics on the minority group refer. If the evaluator promises confidentiality on the survey, then she can only release statistics in the aggregate. The evaluator may be restricted in releasing anecdotes, or telling the "stories," from the data that appear at the individual level.

The traditional school of thought is that the promise of anonymity and confidentiality increases response rates and entices respondents to reveal things that they would not if confidentiality were not promised. Confidentiality and anonymity are often promised, but one should carefully consider whether it is appropriate to do so. For example, a project had the purpose of surveying food programs in rural areas. Its ultimate goal was to provide the funder a map of exactly where each program existed and the nature of each program. The survey could not promise anonymity and confidentiality for questions involving the name and location of a particular food program, as that information was certain to be shared. Also, if maps reflecting the type of program (such as number of users, amount of food distributed, number of volunteers used, and so on) were created, the project could not promise confidentiality for those questions either. Even releasing the names of the sites that provided responses would have violated the promise of anonymity. The evaluators determined that the project would have to present information at a level detailed enough to enable an inquisitive reader to deduce a particular program, so ultimately they decided not to promise confidentiality or anonymity. Given the survey's high response rate, it is not clear that not promising confidentiality and anonymity had any effect in this particular situation. However, if one is collecting sensitive information or information on individuals rather than public institutions, one may need to promise both anonymity and confidentiality to elicit high-quality responses.

Evaluators should be wary about promising anonymity and confidentiality to respondents. If an evaluator makes such promises but later becomes aware via the survey of a situation that appeared unseemly and possibly illegal, would he be able to keep the promise? If collecting information on activities that may be illegal, evaluators may not honestly be able to promise confidentiality.

SUMMARY

This chapter provides an introduction to the many approaches used to collect data. For many small programs, even a new evaluator will be able to conduct informal interviews, run focus groups, and even develop, pretest, and administer a survey. For small programs, sampling may not be an issue because the universe of program participants is not large enough to warrant a sample, so a census will be conducted. For larger programs, the novice evaluator should develop ties with local statisticians to work out kinks in the sample design and possibly to assist in data analysis.

In deciding whether to collect data, the evaluator should first exhaust all existing data sources. Collecting data is expensive and should be undertaken only when there is no alternative. Only data that will actually be useful should be collected, because each additional question on a survey may decrease the response rate. Sampling issues should be carefully considered and before entering into data collection, evaluators should have a clear idea of how each data element will be used to inform the evaluation, how the data element will be used, and who will be the audience for the data element.

It is helpful, even before collecting data, to map out exactly how the information from each question will be used in a report. This exercise saves time and money in the end, because all involved in the evaluation will be better able to see which data will be useful and whether there are questions that evaluators were going to include that ultimately have no place in the report.

Collecting and analyzing data requires time and resources, and at the outset, it is easy to underestimate the amounts needed. Collecting data should be done thoughtfully, with a well-detailed plan of how data collection will proceed, a realistic budget, and a realistic timeline.

When data collection is necessary, then evaluators should consult the program logic model and program theory to determine exactly what information is truly needed to evaluate the program. Data collection should only be done on the outputs and outcomes that have high priority in the PLM and PT.

It may be worthwhile to explore whether any academic centers in your community offer data collection services. With telephone surveys, data collectors do not even need to be local, so places like the University of Pittsburgh's Center for Social and Urban Research and Quinnipiac University's Survey Research Center may be able to help design the survey, conduct the telephone interviews, and create the database (for a fee, of course). An experienced center already equipped with the necessary technology may ultimately be an economical approach to collecting the data.

KEY TERMS

anonymity

CATI system

census

confidentiality

convenience sample

focus group

formal survey instrument

informal interviews

interviewer-administered surveys

psychological pretesting

question reliability

question validity

sample

sampling error

self-administered surveys

simple random sample

snowball sample

stratified random sample

DISCUSSION QUESTIONS

1. If you are the leader of a focus group, why should you *not* be concerned if you don't get through all of your questions?

2. Why is it important to offer open-ended questions to a focus group, but not in a survey?

3. Discuss the benefits and drawbacks of offering confidentiality to survey respondents.

CHAPTER

CONCLUSIONS

LEARNING OBJECTIVES

After reading this chapter, you should be able to

- Explain how the evaluation report can mirror grant proposals
- Understand what makes an appropriate evaluation

Toward the early part of this text, I introduced Carol Weiss's outline of the evaluation report. I invite you to revisit that outline. By this time, you should be able to conceptualize what a reasonable evaluation plan would be for a given program or policy.

USING EVALUATION TOOLS TO DEVELOP GRANT PROPOSALS

In my course on program evaluation, I assign the graduate students to nonprofits and businesses for whom they are to design an evaluation plan. (There usually isn't time within a semester to learn about program evaluation and collect all of the information that may be necessary to carry out the plan.) At the beginning of the course, I review issues surrounding the creation of appropriate evaluation questions. In theory, forming the evaluation questions is not difficult. But when dealing with real people, students inevitably are challenged by the task of forming evaluation questions.

In working with agencies, I have found that the stage of forming and defining the evaluation question is really the key to creating a good, useful, and appropriate evaluation. Once you have developed your evaluator's toolbox by understanding issues of causation, the various quasi-experimental designs, and trade-offs between threats to the different types of validity, then two points remain: (1) What is the program? and (2) What are the relevant evaluation questions?

The first question can only be answered by rigorously describing the program via the program logic model and program theory. The second question requires the most thought. Remember that evaluation questions are a function both of the desires of the various stakeholders and of a thorough understanding of the literature surrounding the program's activities and theory.

With the evaluator's tools developed, I contend that the art of evaluation becomes an art of listening, understanding, and developing a sense of how value can be added by the research that the evaluator will be conducting. The best evaluation may not be the most appropriate. The most appropriate evaluation is the one that will provide usable information that will eventually be acted upon to improve the program. It will be the source of policy and programmatic recommendations. If inappropriate, the best evaluation runs the risk of being overlooked and irrelevant. Evaluators must have good listening skills in addition to their other skills.

I encourage every evaluator to retain a good dose of skepticism throughout his evaluation career. Evaluators must remain doubtful of the claims of both supporters and critics of programs. I am afraid that once an evaluator becomes enmeshed in a programmatic area, she risks losing that healthy degree of skepticism. Without skepticism, an evaluator no longer doubts whether the program can be effective, and ends up asking (and answering) either the wrong questions or questions that do not get at the heart of the issue.

In the current state of evaluation, there is a critical mass of evaluators who see evaluation holistically and as a way to benefit programs and processes, but there remains a tendency for "evaluations" to end with measuring what are called program outcomes. Sometimes, outcomes get measured without regard to ultimately attributing changes in the outcomes to a program's activities.

Funders have an even more difficult task in using evaluations than do program personnel. Not only should funders be asking about the effects of the programs that they help to fund, but they should also ask whether the programs were effective because of their contributions.

Nearly all funders now require, as part of the grant proposal, a statement of how the agency plans to evaluate the program. The sections of an evaluation report, presented in Chapter Three, nearly coincide with the sections of a good grant proposal. A good grant proposal will first discuss the problem that the program addresses; the size, scope, seriousness of the problem; trends in the problem over time; and prior efforts to deal with the problem. These sections come first because the agency wants to motivate funders to solve the problem. Then, the proposal will rigorously describe the program. If a program logic model and program theory are used to describe the program, the funder is likely to be impressed. Using a PLM and PT shows the funder that the applicant has thought seriously about the program, and this gives funders more confidence in the program. If there are any unintentional negative effects that could result, an applicant is wise to bring these up here and frankly discuss why these are not serious threats to the program's success, rather than letting the funder's board members think of possible unintended negative impacts on their own. An applicant should present the context for the program and, if possible, show that the community supports the program.

The rest of the grant proposal will be written in the subjunctive and future tenses—will, would, intend, expect, should. Applicants should discuss the number of clients that they expect the program to serve and the length of time clients are expected to interact with the program.

Applicants should also present an evaluation plan—what the central questions of evaluation activities will be, how processes will be examined, what sort of outputs and outcomes are expected, and finally, how they intend to show that changes in outcomes are attributable to the program. If the program will not be considering attribution, then the applicants should be frank about this, which will increase the program's credibility and show that the program is aware of evaluation issues. Finally, the proposal should show how the program intends to use the information collected to continuously improve.

The more detailed the proposal can be about the program and its evaluation, the more credible the application will appear and the greater the likelihood of it being funded. Of course, a sensible, transparent budget will reveal to the funder how the program intends to use the monies the funder grants to the program.

If a funder does not yet require a rigorous description of a program, any agency that rigorously describes the program as recommended above will stand out as exemplary in the grant reviewing process. It is likely that if a grant proposal nearly follows the sections of the evaluation report as described here, it will be looked upon favorably. The funders will know that the agency has thought hard and carefully about the program.

HIRING AN EVALUATION CONSULTANT

I do not expect everybody who has read this book to become evaluators. I hope that this text has provided you with enough background to become an "educated consumer" of evaluation consultants. Many readers will immediately or eventually hire or work with an evaluator. Evaluation consultants should be asked how they will describe the program, what literature they will review, what quasi-experimental design they expect to use, who will own the evaluation, and how they will collect data. Many consultants who call themselves "outcome" consultants have trouble seeing programs holistically. They focus on outcomes, even when the strong literature behind a program suggests that evaluation activities should focus on processes.

Before hiring an evaluation consultant, you should think through exactly what you want the consultant to do. I have seen organizations hand over to consultants all aspects of a summative evaluation, only to find that the report did not answer what in the organization's eyes were the most fundamental questions about the program. I have also met people who claimed that they were evaluators but did not have the skills to carry out an evaluation. There has been a tendency for some evaluators to not review the literature around a program, thus increasing the number of evaluation questions and resulting in unnecessarily elevated costs.

Any organization hiring an evaluator should think about what the structure of the evaluation activities will be. For large projects, I recommend that if the organization does not have the expertise on hand to supervise the evaluation consultant, it should engage someone with such expertise. In the home remodeling arena, one can hire a "construction manager" to oversee a contractor. Similarly, for large evaluations, an organization would be well-served to have an "evaluation manager."

I encourage those in nonprofits, government agencies, and international NGOs to reach out to their local academics to assist in evaluation activities and even in the development of programs. Academics may have time to assist in evaluation. The collaboration could benefit both the academics and the programs, for academics are often eager to participate in "real world" activities and the programs will receive advice from someone who isn't fully dependent on consulting income, which could mean that the academics will be more willing to provide unbiased advice. The American Evaluation Association is a good resource for identifying evaluators and their affiliations in a local area.

I have seen that the power of evaluation is strongest when evaluation activities are built into a program's design. It serves a program well to identify and work with an evaluator starting at the program's conception.

SUMMARY

Forming and defining evaluation questions is the key to creating a good, useful, and appropriate evaluation. The most appropriate evaluation is not necessarily the best evaluation but the one that will be acted upon. Evaluation has the most impact when evaluation activities are included in the design of a program.

KEY TERMS

causation

evaluation plan

evaluation report

program logic model

program theory

quasi-experimental design

stakeholders

DISCUSSION QUESTIONS

1. Describe the parallels of the evaluation report and a grant proposal.

2. What are the keys to an appropriate evaluation?

3. Why is it important to be able to look at a program holistically?

APPENDIX

AMERICAN COMMUNITY SURVEY

In 2000, the U.S. Census Bureau administered two surveys to the entire population of the United States. Most households received the "short form," but a small sample of households were asked to complete the "long form." These forms are useful in that they show exactly how questions on commonly used demographic indicators were worded.

Readers can see the short form at www.census.gov/dmd/www/pdf/d61a.pdf. The long form can be viewed at www.census.gov/dmd/www/pdf/d02p.pdf.

If an agency is going to collect demographic data on its clients with the goal of comparing them with the population of the entire service area, for example, or the population of the United States, the agency should use the same wording of the relevant question as was used on the last U.S. Census.

Starting in 2000, the U.S. Census Bureau began implementing the "American Community Survey." This survey is to replace the data that the long form uniquely collected. Information on the American Community Survey, including questionnaires used for it, can be found at www.census.gov/acs/www.

GLOSSARY

activities. What a program actually does, activities the public may witness and those that occur behind the scenes; often includes how clients are recruited, how staff is trained, how the program reaches the target population, and how the program interacts with its clients.

anonymity. The link between an individual's responses and the individual's name will be broken.

archival data. Data collected in the past; also called historical data.

assumptions. How a program perceives the environment in which it operates.

categorical data. Data collected in terms of categories.

CATI system. Computer Assisted Telephone Interview system; an interviewer reads questions from a computer screen and enters responses directly into the computer, which typically creates a database of responses.

causation. To bring about change.

census. Data collection from 100 percent of the units in the universe.

cohort. A group which experienced the same event at the same time.

compensatory equalization. When the control group receives either the actual treatment or some version of it.

compensatory rivalry. The control group behaves abnormally well to show they are better than the treatment group.

confidentiality. Data will be held in confidence and used appropriately.

construct validity. Degree to which the theoretical constructs have been well-specified and both the cause and effect constructs have been appropriately operationalized.

continuous data. Raw, non-categorical data; allows for the most flexibility in data analysis.

continuous effects. Effects that last forever.

convenience sample. Created at the convenience of the data collectors; not a formal sampling approach.

delayed treatment control group design. Where the control group eventually receives the treatment, but at a later date than the "treatment" group; sometimes known as "switching replications design."

different samples design. Also called sampling without replacement; drawing pretest samples from the treatment and control groups that have different individuals than posttest samples.

diffusion of a treatment. Treatment and control groups overlap or share information.

discontinuous effects. Short-lived effects; impacts that wear off with time.

evaluation. Done to examine whether a program or policy causes a change; assists with continuous programmatic improvement and introspection.

evaluation plan. Consists of what the central questions of evaluation activities will be, how processes will be examined, what sort of outputs and outcomes are expected, and how the program intends to show that changes in outcomes are attributable to the program.

evaluation report. After research is done on an intervention, a report is written and disseminated to relevant stakeholders.

evaluator. The person who performs or studies evaluations.

external evaluator. Evaluator hired on a contractual basis; has the appearance of impartiality.

external validity. The generalizability of the relationship found in one evaluation or study to other people, places, and contexts.

false negative conclusion. False conclusion that a causal relationship does not exist when, in fact, there is a causal relationship.

false positive conclusion. False conclusion that a causal relationship does exist, when, in fact, there is not a causal relationship.

fishing. Throwing all possible variables into an analysis and letting the statistical analysis reveal what variables show statistical significance.

focus group. A group of people who can reveal their thoughts, attitudes, and experiences about an issue. Used to discover the issues that exist and range of circumstances and views.

formal survey instrument. Used to discover the frequency of issues and views.

formative evaluation. Produces information that is fed back to decision makers who can use it to continuously improve the program; often referred to as "evaluatory activities."

goals. Change(s) that the program anticipates will result from the intervention's activities.

high stakes evaluations. Outcome-based evaluations used as the basis for making important decisions about the survival of a program.

high stakes testing. Occurs when test results are used to make decisions that have large ramifications; can lead to a weak evaluation and distort behavior around the test.

informal interview. Conversation with stakeholders done initially to understand the program.

inputs. What it takes to operate the program, including monetary funding, in-kind contributions, physical space, characteristics and qualifications of staff, and particular expertise of staff.

internal evaluator. Usually on the staff of the program's organization; has familiarity with the organization, sometimes the particular program being evaluated; may have an understanding of the personalities within the organization.

internal validity. The degree to which the study has shown that a causal relationship exists.

intervening variable. Factors other than cause and effect whose presence or absence can cloud the true relationship a program has with outcomes.

interviewer-administered survey. Conducted in person in a face-to-face interview or over the phone.

iterative process. Multiple rounds of examining and crafting before the final.

lagged effect. Delay before effect appears, not immediate; the time delay makes the effects difficult to attribute to the intervention.

longitudinal data. Data from the same unit over consecutive periods of time.

measurement error. The degree of imprecision in measures.

mono-method bias. Only one measure is used to reflect a theoretical construct.

mono-operation bias. Various measurements are presented in the same way.

necessary. The only way the desired outcome could occur is if the intervention caused it to occur.

necessary and sufficient. The outcome can only be produced by the program or intervention, and if one went through the program the outcome would always be produced.

negatively covary. Increase in the causes would be associated with an observed decrease in the effect, and vice versa.

nonequivalent groups using switched measures. Total group of people who receive the treatment are divided into two subgroups; the first observation of one subgroup is the outcome measure A, and the first subgroup's second observation is of the outcome measure B; for the second group, B is the first measure and A the second.

nonequivalent observations design drawn from one group. Uses the same people in the treatment group as the control group; conducts measurements on only a single group of persons.

observable differences. Differences in demographic characteristics.

one-group posttest-only design. Quasi-experimental design where only the outcomes of the participant group are examined at only one time—after the program.

one-group pretest-posttest design. Quasi-experimental design where the treatment group is measured with a single pretest and a single posttest.

operationalize. Brings a theoretical concept down to the practical realm.

outcome evaluation. Emphasizes the change in clients or participants that resulted from the program's activities.

outcome measures. Quantitatively reflects the measures, counts, rates, or indicators used to operationalize articulated outcomes.

outcomes. The desired impact of the program using words, not numbers; usually relate to the program's goals.

outputs. Measures that show the program is actually operating.

parsimony. The smallest set that will deliver the most bang for the buck.

period effects. The passage of time affects the identical program in two different time periods.

permanency of effect. The length of time an effect is present, long-lasting vs. short-lived.

positively covary. Increase in the cause would be associated with an increase in the effect.

posttest-only design with nonequivalent groups. Quasi-experimental design where the outcomes of two groups, the participant group and the control group, are examined only after the program.

primary goals. Primary reasons for the program's existence; goals the program must achieve.

process evaluation. Focuses on program processes—the "how" of program delivery processes.

program implementation model. Reflects the sequence of a program's activities, akin to a flow chart.

program logic model (PLM). Models the operation of the program and the logic behind it; details how the program is operating, with what resources, whom it targets, what it intends to accomplish; consists of eight columns: (1) goals, (2) assumptions, (3) target population, (4) inputs, (5) activities, (6) outputs, (7) outcomes, (8) outcome measures.

program theory. A diagram of the theory behind the program, sometimes called theory of change.

psychological pretesting. The respondent talks about how s/he is thinking about the questions as s/he is taking the survey.

publication bias. Evaluations that show that programs have impacts are more likely to be published than those that show programs have no effect, are poorly implemented, or show conflicting results.

quasi-experimental design. A way to examine qualitative data in a structured way.

quasi-experimental notation. A way to display the quasi-experimental design where "O" indicates an observation and "X" indicates an intervention or treatment [introduced by Cook & Campbell (1979)].

question reliability. The extent to which people in comparable situations will respond to questions in similar ways; also the extent to which the same respondent in unchanged circumstances will respond to the same questions in the same way.

question validity. The extent to which a given response reflects what the survey designer intends and expects the response to mean.

resentful demoralization. The control group behaves abnormally poorly.

sample. A collection of data from less than 100 percent of the units in the universe.

sampling error. The extent to which the sample estimate varies from the population estimate.

secondary goals. Goals a program has but which are not the primary reason for the program's existence.

simple random sample. There must be a list from which to draw sampled units; every unit on the list has the same chance of being entered into the sample; units are selected by chance to be in the sample.

small sample size. Sample size of less than fifty units; conclusions from small sample sizes can be unreliable.

snowball sample. The sample grows because of referrals from people already in the sample.

spectacular causes. In a tipping point situation, a large dose of the cause (program or intervention) produces small effects.

spectacular effects. In a tipping point situation, a small dose of the cause (program or intervention) produces very large effects.

stakeholders. People who have an interest in the program, such as program administrators, funders, boards of directors, clients, staff, advocates, and alumni.

statistical conclusion validity. The appropriateness of the statistical techniques used for the analysis.

stratified random sample. Separating the sample and assigning different probabilities of being selected.

sufficient. The program will absolutely procedure the intended outcome.

summative evaluation. A "report card" evaluation; information produced is used to determine the extent of the program's effectiveness; often takes the form of evaluation reports.

target population. The units of analysis or population that the program or intervention intends to impact.

targets or benchmarks. Measurements by which program success is defined.

threat of history. An event that could affect the level of the outcome indicator, independent of the program's influence; occurs during the time between the start and end of the program when something that would independently exert an influence on the program's outcomes occurs during the program's operation but outside of the program.

threat of instrumentation. Means of data collection changes between pre-intervention and post-intervention observations, and this change affects the quantification of the observation.

threat of maturation. Some participants may have changed in the way that the program intends them to just because time passed.

threat of mortality. Those who dropped out of the program differ from those who stayed in and completed the program.

threat of selection. When participation is voluntary, it is likely that those who participate in the program differ in some way from those who do not participate.

threat of statistical regression. A program is offered only to those who have performed exceptionally well or poorly on a pretest, and their posttest observation is likely to be closer to the mean of all units who were pre-tested.

threat of testing. Responses on a test change as familiarity with the test increases.

threats to validity. Events or circumstances that have the potential to make conclusions based on the research invalid in a certain respect.

time series. Follow the same "unit" over time.

type I error. Evaluator concludes the outcomes of various treatment groups differ, when in reality they do not.

type II error. Evaluator concludes the outcomes of the various treatment groups do not differ, when in reality they do.

unit of analysis. What the program aims to affect; the "thing" to which the outcome measure applies.

untreated control group design with pretest and posttest. Quasi-experimental design that includes both a participant and control group and two observations—one pre-treatment and one post-treatment.

validity. Extent to which there has been an approximation of truth.

REFERENCES

American Evaluation Association. *Position Statement on High Stakes Testing in PreK-12 Education.* AEA Task Force, February 2002. Available at http://www.eval.org/hst3.htm.

Bickman, L., and Hamner, K. "An Evaluation of the Yad Vashem Holocaust Museum." *Evaluation Review,* 1998, 22(4), 435–446.

Cook, T., and Campbell, D. *Quasi-Experimentation: Design and Analysis Issues for Field Settings.* Boston: Houghton Mifflin, 1979.

Daponte, B. O., and Bade, S. *The Evolution, Cost, and Operation of the Private Food Assistance Network.* September 2000. Institute for Research on Poverty, Discussion Papers. DP# 1211-00.

Daponte, B. O., Sanders, S., and Taylor, L. "Why Do Eligible Households Not Use Food Stamps? Evidence from an Experiment." *Journal of Human Resources,* 1999, 34(3), 612–628.

David, H., and Wright, N. "Abortion Legislation: The Romanian Experience." *Studies in Family Planning,* 1971, 2(10), 205–210.

Gill, B., Dembosky, J., and Caulkins, J, A *"Noble Bet" in Early Care and Education: Lessons from One Community's Experience.* Pittsburgh, Pa.: Rand, 2002. Available at www.rand.org/publications/MR/MR1544.

Lieberson, *S. Making It Count: The Improvement of Social Research and Theory.* Berkeley: University of California Press, 1985.

Patton, M. Q. "A World Larger than Formative and Summative." *Evaluation Practice,* 1996, 17(2), 131–144.

U.S. Department of Agriculture, Center for Nutrition Policy and Promotion. *Thrifty Food Plan,* Administrative Report. Washington, D.C.: USDA, 1999.

W. K. Kellogg Foundation. *W. K. Kellogg Foundation Evaluation Handbook,* 1998. Available at www.wkkf.org/Pubs/Tools/Evaluation/Pub770.pdf.

W. K. Kellogg Foundation. *W. K. Kellogg Foundation Logic Model Development Guide,* 2001, 1–26. Available at www.wkkf.org/Pubs/Tools/Evaluation/Pub3669.pdf.

Weiss, C. H. *Evaluation: Methods for Studying Programs and Policies.* (2nd ed.) Englewood Cliffs, N.J.: Prentice-Hall, 1998.

INDEX

165